"My eyes are awake before the watches of the night, that I may meditate upon thy promise."

PSALM 119:148

p. 144

THE PROMISE

Cardinal Jean-Marie Lustiger

Translated from the French by
Rebecca Howell Balinski,
Msgr. Richard Malone,
and Jean Duchesne

Revised by Rivka Karplus
under the supervision of the author

WILLIAM B. EERDMANS PUBLISHING COMPANY
GRAND RAPIDS, MICHIGAN / CAMBRIDGE, U.K.

Originally published in French as *La Promesse*
© 2002 Editions Parole et Silence
English translation © 2007 Jean-Marie Lustiger
All rights reserved

Published 2007 by
Wm. B. Eerdmans Publishing Co.
2140 Oak Industrial Drive N.E., Grand Rapids, Michigan 49505 /
P.O. Box 163, Cambridge CB3 9PU U.K.
www.eerdmans.com

Printed in the United States of America

12 11 10 09 08 07   7 6 5 4 3 2 1

Library of Congress Cataloging-in-Publication Data

Lustiger, Jean-Marie, 1926–2007
[La Promesse. English]
The promise / Cardinal Jean-Marie Lustiger;
translated from the French by Rebecca Howell Balinski,
Msgr. Richard Malone, and Jean Duchesne; revised by Rivka Karplus.
p.   cm.
Includes bibliographical references and index.
ISBN 978-0-8028-0771-7 (pbk.: alk. paper)
1. Jesus Christ — Messiahship.   2. Israel (Christian theology)
3. Christianity and other religions — Judaism.
4. Judaism — Relations — Christianity.   I. Title.

BT230.L8713   2007
231.7′6 — dc22

2007027524

Contents

Contents

Contents

Foreword

Translated by Rebecca Howell Balinski

In 1979, I had served for ten years as a priest in the parish of Sainte-Jeanne de Chantal in Paris. Cardinal François Marty, Archbishop of Paris, had appointed me to remain there until 1981. I dreamed of taking some time afterwards, with my bishop's permission, to pray, reflect, and live in the Holy Land. This dream of mine is presently being realized by Cardinal Carlo Maria Martini, Archbishop emeritus of Milan.

It is difficult after twenty-four years of progress brought about under the pontificate of John Paul II to imagine what the "mentality" of Catholics, both priests and lay persons, as well as the public in general, was like beforehand. The decade following 1968 was truly a strange period! In the mid 1970s the silence regarding the deportation of Jews — regarding what was initially called the Holocaust and then the Shoah — was finally broken in France.

In 1975 — or '76 — I had gone to the Bec-Hellouin Abbey for a time of prayer. It had been a great joy for me to meet Dom Grammont, the abbot, who at that time told me about his intention to send several monks to reestablish monastic life at the Abu Gosh Abbey in Israel. Among those whose mission it would be to integrate the community into the contemporary life of the country was a young man, Brother Jean-Baptiste, who would subsequently become the abbot of the new foundation.

After the end of World War II, several major religious orders had attempted similar experiences in Israel. Heroic endeavors, which had been quickly put to the test. The Bec-Hellouin project had impressed me, because it was to be based on the humble and peaceful prayer of a few monks. I had expressed my feelings to Dom Grammont, whose wise and audacious initiatives for Christian unity and relations with the Jewish people I much admired.

* * *

This is no doubt the reason that the nuns at Sainte Françoise Romaine — a convent twinned with Bec-Hellouin, and among whose community were several women I had known as students at the Sorbonne — later asked me to preach a week-long retreat and help them to pray and reflect on the mystery of Israel.

This request amazed and deeply moved me. For the first time in my life, I was asked to broach this subject within the prayer of a contemplative community. I knew that in speaking to these nuns, I would not have to be on guard against tactless or indiscreet curiosity. I would not be subjected to the suspicions, prejudices, or wounding reactions that speaking in public can provoke. A completely shared faith made a reciprocal confidence possible. This true communion freed both my mind and heart. I knew that what I would be able to say would nourish their prayer. First and foremost, in speaking to them, I would have to share the riches received from the grace of God.

I gratefully accepted their invitation, which I felt to be a call from God; and which, for myself, was a God-given grace.

Just prior to this retreat I had participated in a patient and continuous study of Saint Matthew's Gospel, which thus became the starting point for these talks.

* * *

Speaking freely and improvising, I let myself be guided from day to day by an interior logic whose source was the text of the Gospel. At times, the restraint imposed by speech could give an overly theoretical aspect to my remarks. Most often, however, I openly shared my meditation, because I felt assured that it was falling on sympathetic ears and, in the secret of God, could eventually bear fruit for the Church, since it was being deposited in the silence of the community's prayer.

I did not keep any notes from these talks nor do I have a precise memory of how they developed. With my approval, the nuns had taped my remarks, which were subsequently transcribed. I had requested that this transcription, which did not really constitute a finished text, be limited to their personal use. I am well aware of the shortcuts, incoherencies, and approximations of improvised speech on particularly difficult subjects, especially when this speech is wrested from heart and spirit, often searching for the words themselves. The nuns promised to honor my request and I think they kept their word.

Then, for a long time, I heard nothing more about the text. Nevertheless, I had to consent to have it transmitted — always with the same reservations — to other contemplative communities, in particular, to those in the Holy Land.

*   *   *

And then, two or three years ago, these pages, which had traveled much farther than I could ever have imagined, reappeared! Several friends, including a publisher, besieged me with arguments that they should be made available to a broader public. All possible reasons were advanced to overcome my reluctance. After a long hesitation, I came around to their point of view.

I forced myself to reread the text and remove the most visible traces of the oral style and a train of thought still seeking to formulate itself. However, still not completely convinced, I bowed to the insistent request and left the text in its "unpolished, unstructured" state. I have not eliminated the repetitions of a speaker who seeks to make himself understood, who adjusts his remarks as he considers them.

I entrust to an extended and unknown audience words originally addressed to a religious community who received them benevolently in prayer. I wish to thank the Paris Cathedral School for providing the footnotes that will assist the reader in following the thoughts expressed in these pages.

*   *   *

In rereading the transcripts of these talks, I was surprised by what I had said — or rather, at what my audience had allowed me to say, by its trust and receptivity. I was surprised because, more than twenty years later, I discovered that many thoughts expressed almost in an undertone — sometimes passionately, sometimes hesitatingly — appear to have timidly foreshadowed what the logic of the faith and life of the Church would produce thanks to the initiative of John Paul II.

Hence the decision to propose these thoughts to the general reader, and to add the texts of speeches successively given when I was invited in 1995 by the University of Tel Aviv, then in 2002 by the European Jewish Congress (in Paris), the World Jewish Congress (in Brussels), and the American Jewish Committee (in Washington, D.C.), at the end of the book.

Rereading the talks given to Jewish audiences in the light of the 1979 retreat enabled me to measure the distance traveled. The circumstances and nature of the texts, admittedly, are diametrically opposed. In 1979 I was speaking as a priest and friend to a community of Catholic nuns, in the mutual trust of a shared meditation. In 1995 and 2002, I was responding to invitations from eminent Jewish organizations that had acknowledged the work of John Paul II and asked me to witness to it. It seemed to me, however, that the more recent reflections did not lessen the value of the earlier ones, and that they even might shed some light on them.

To those who are made uncomfortable by the time gap between 1979 and the turn of the third millennium, I can only answer that what is expressed here is only a part of what I have experienced, thought, written, and published on the subject in the interim. Moreover, what I have said over the years has always been shaped by the circumstances for which my words were solicited, sometimes for specialized, often foreign, journals unknown to the public at large. Also, I have explicitly taken up the same crucial subjects, in quite different contexts and perspectives, in *Dare to Believe* (1985) and *Choosing God* (1987), and they have inevitably reappeared in the digressions of at least a dozen other books published in the interval.

I am well aware of the risk taken in making these words available to readers who might not be as kindly disposed to me as the audiences I addressed in 1979, then in 1995 and 2002. Certain passages in the first part might seem excessive or even disconcerting to Jewish readers, and certain passages in the second part, disconcerting or even excessive to Catholic readers.

May both groups grant that I have acted in good faith, in the service of the Word of God given to mankind for the happiness and salvation of all.

"Lord, now lettest thou thy servant depart in peace,

according to thy word;

for mine eyes have seen thy salvation

which thou hast prepared in the presence of all peoples,

a light for revelation to the Gentiles,

and for glory to thy people Israel."

Luke 2:29-32

1979

*Talks given at the Convent of Sainte Françoise Romaine
of the Bec-Hellouin Abbey*

Translated by Rebecca Howell Balinski

CHAPTER 1

Jesus and the Law

The Church appears in Jerusalem, after Pentecost, as an "assembly," *kahal* in Hebrew, *ecclesia* in Greek. It is unthinkable that she would claim to replace Israel.[1] She is not another Israel, but the very fulfillment, in Israel, of God's plan. The Church — that of the Messiah, Jesus — is originally the Church of Jerusalem as described in the Acts of the Apostles. It was to be the "Mother-Church" and would experience the promises made to Israel and given in Christ: in the Messiah, the grace given to Israel becomes accessible to pagans. In the words used by Luke in his Gospel (Luke 2:32), the elderly Simeon foretells that the child Jesus will be "a light for revelation to the Gentiles, and for glory to thy people Israel." Thus, when this hope is accomplished, the pagan nations accede to the Election of Israel and share in its grace.

The Church is then faced with the question of the extent to which these pagans who share in Israel's Election should be obliged to observe the laws which are Israel's trust, responsibility, and privilege. To what extent should these pagans be associated with the totality of Is-

1. In the context of these talks, "Israel" designates the Jewish people according to the blessing granted by God; cf. Genesis 32:29; 35:10. The words refer to the State of Israel only when clearly indicated.

5

rael's mission? This is the major problem facing the first generation of Christians, as all the New Testament writings testify.

The "Catholic" Church

The Church appears as "catholic," to use a term which will later be adopted, meaning "according to the whole." She is "according to the whole" because she is composed of both Jews and pagans. She fulfills the mystery of the salvation of all nations because she brings together the two groups according to whom history is divided: those who participate in the Election, Israel, and those who had no right to it, the pagans. For both groups, salvation is given as a grace, and a grace unmerited.

This Church is "according to the whole," since this "assembly of God" is formed from among both Jews and pagans. She can exist as a Church only within the mystery of the grace given to Israel. In this mystery, the pagans have to recognize a gift which is freely given to them, through no merit of their own. Reciprocally, by recognizing God's gift to the pagans, Israel has to acknowledge that what it has received is not its due, but a grace of God.

In this mystery of reciprocal recognition of God's freely given grace, each party bears witness to the other. Each attests that God's gift is absolutely unmerited, and each enables the other to realize the universality of sin, since sin can only be fully perceived in light of God's mercy. Because God has been completely merciful toward Israel, Israel can in turn discover that the same grace is given to the pagans; and if the pagans recognize the freely given gift they receive in being permitted to share God's gift to Israel, the grace of God is made manifest in its full splendor.

In this early Church, the status of the Pagan-Christian assemblies begins to be established. They are not dispensed from observing the Law — if the pagans did not observe the Law, they would have no share in either Israel's Election or grace. But the gift of the Holy Spirit, a grace of the Messiah, enables pagans to observe the Law differently from Israel, which remains charged with this "delightful" burden of observance.[2]

The Church of Jerusalem is, in the Catholic Church, the permanence of the promise made to Israel, the presence of the fulfillment of that promise, an attestation of the grace bestowed on the pagans. Thus, the Church is that of both Jews and pagans.

The fact that this Church of Jerusalem was to survive only until the sixth century is one of history's great mysteries and may well be a great spiritual tragedy — whose final outcome remains hidden. For this matter, like the separation of the Church into Eastern and Western branches, cannot be considered settled.[3] These mysteries are a part of the wounds, the sins, that we must acknowledge, which judge us and where we must wait for God to act according to his promise.

The Jerusalem Church, destroyed under Byzantine pressure, was undoubtedly a major loss for the Christian conscience. The memory of the grace bestowed was thus practically erased — not by the Church, as the bride of Christ, but by Christians. This became for them a source of temptation and a spiritual trial, a cause for unfaithfulness to Christ. Herein lies one of the major problems of Christianity.

Going Up to Jerusalem

These reflections are not unrelated to the relationship between Jesus and the Law. To understand it, we must reread the Gospel written by Saint Matthew, the evangelist who was the most sensitive to this question.

Let us begin with the episode concerning the "rich young man" (Matthew 19:16), which occurs when Jesus is on his way to Jerusalem.

From the moment he sets out on this journey, obstacles and ob-

2. "Thy law is my delight" (Psalm 119:174; see also 119:24). The Law is often compared to the "yoke" placed on the shoulders of an animal; cf. Zephaniah 3:9; Jeremiah 2:20 and Sirach 51:26. Jesus takes up the image: "For my yoke is easy, and my burden is light" (cf. Matthew 11:30).

3. The separation occurred in 1054. In 1439, the Council of Florence, known as the "Council of Union," was an attempt at reconciliation.

jections abound. The first question focuses on the relationship between man and woman: "Is it lawful to divorce one's wife for any cause?" Jesus answers by referring to Genesis: "What God hath joined together, let not man put asunder." However, everything concerning marriage in the Law is to be understood also — and perhaps, above all — as concerning the union of God and Israel. In Saint Paul's reasoning, marriage is revealed as the sacrament of God's union with his People, and not the inverse.[4] In other words, it is not human love that sheds light on the mystery of God, it is the mystery of God that makes it possible to understand something of human love and which gives Israel its true vocation for its human behavior. Jesus' response refers to God's Covenant with his people: "What God hath joined together, let not man put asunder." Thus, it applies to Israel and the indissolubility of God's promise.

Next comes Christ's appeal for absolute detachment, followed by his welcome of the little children despite his disciples' protests.

"What Good Thing Shall I Do?" — "Follow Me"

Then the rich young man arrived: "And behold, one came up to him, saying: 'Teacher, what good deed must I do, to have eternal life?' And he said to him, 'Why do you ask me about what is good? One there is who is good. If you would enter life, keep the commandments.' He said to him, 'Which?' And Jesus said, 'You shall not kill, you shall not commit adultery, you shall not steal, you shall not bear false witness, honor your father and mother — in short, you shall love your neighbor as yourself.' The young man said to him, 'All these I have observed; what do I still lack?' Jesus said to him, 'If you would be perfect, go, sell what you possess and give to the poor, and you will have treasure in heaven; and come, follow me.' When the young man heard this he went away sorrowful; for he had great possessions. And Jesus said to his disciples, 'Truly, I say to you, it will be hard for a rich man to enter the kingdom

4. Cf. Ephesians 5:21-32.

of heaven. Again I tell you, it is easier for a camel to go through the eye of a needle than for a rich man to enter the kingdom of God.' When the disciples heard this they were greatly astonished, saying, 'Who then can be saved?' But Jesus looked at them and said to them, 'With men this is impossible, but with God all things are possible.'"

The way in which Jesus quotes the commandments seems strange. If we refer to Exodus or Deuteronomy, we see that Jesus omits the first half. He begins with "You shall not kill, you shall not commit adultery, you shall not steal, you shall not bear false witness," and he follows these commandments with "Honor your father and your mother."[5] That is, he goes back to a previous commandment.

One of the simplest explanations lies in the disposition of the Ten Commandments.[6] Normally they appear in two parallel series on two Tables, with the words "Honor your father and your mother" coming at the end of the first Table, after the first four commandments which concern God. Thus, Jesus begins with the second Table and returns to the first by starting from the bottom.

Such an explanation is possible. But it remains strange that the first commandments, the most important ones, should not be cited. In fact, I believe that they are deliberately mentioned, and that they are, indeed, the major focus of this text. The pursuit of Christ — the "follow me" — is the way Jesus proposes for fulfilling the commandments of the first Table, the commandments concerning God.

The way that Jesus proposes for observing these commandments — by telling the young man to give away all his possessions and become his disciple — refers us directly to the *Shema Israel* (Deuteronomy 6:4): "Hear, O Israel: the LORD our God is one LORD; and you shall love the LORD your God with all your heart, and with all your soul, and with all your might."[7] These words were commonly interpreted by the sages

---

5. Cf. Exodus 20:2-17; Deuteronomy 5:6-21.

6. The Ten Commandments or *ten words* are presented on two Tables; cf. Exodus 32:15; 34:1-4-29. They can be found at the end of the chapter.

7. The complete text of Deuteronomy 6:4-9 should be read: "Hear, O Israel: The LORD our God is one LORD; and you shall love the LORD your God with all your heart,

of the time as meaning "with all your means," thus including "all your possessions."

To love God with all one's might is not to be interpreted merely in the metaphorical sense. It means concretely: "with everything you possess." We are to give everything to God. Jesus' response evokes this phrase from Deuteronomy and lends it an eminently practical meaning. He says to the young man, "Very well, sell all you have! Love God with all your resources — then you will observe the first commandments. And the only way to do this is to follow me." For Jesus is the fulfillment of the Law.

What then is the Christian vocation? What is the vocation of perfection that leads to eternal life and makes us perfect as the Heavenly Father is perfect? It is to observe the totality of the commandments. Jesus is the one who fulfills these commandments to perfection and gives strength to those who follow him so that they, too, can fulfill them perfectly.

We have the confirmation that this passage must be read in this way in Jesus' last arguments in the Temple. These confrontations are a test, the supreme temptation before that of his Passion. In chapter 22 of Saint Matthew, Jesus is subjected to a triple temptation from his interlocutors: (1) the tribute due to Caesar; (2) the woman with seven husbands — a temptation that focuses on the Sadducees' interpretation of the Law as regards the resurrection, a literal interpretation rather than one related to the meaning of the resurrection as a gift of life; and finally, (3) what is the greatest commandment? The temptation consists precisely in choosing among the commandments.

---

and with all your soul, and with all your might. And these words which I command you this day shall be upon your heart; and you shall teach them diligently to your children, and shall talk of them when you sit in your house, and when you walk by the way, and when you lie down, and when you rise. And you shall bind them as a sign upon your hand, and they shall be as frontlets between your eyes. And you shall write them on the doorposts of your house and on your gates."

The Greatest Commandment

It is the third temptation that must be kept in mind. I have used the word *temptation* because Saint Matthew himself places it in Jesus' mouth regarding the tribute to be rendered to Caesar: "Why do you tempt me, you hypocrites?" A little later, in verse 35, the evangelist says: "And one of them a lawyer, asked him a question, to tempt him." The expression is usually translated "put to the test," or "held in a trap," etc. But the word is exactly the same as the one used for Christ's temptation in the wilderness. There is an explicit reference to that same reality. Here, the temptation is to choose the "greatest commandment" within the Law. Jesus replies, "You shall love the Lord your God with all your heart, and with all your soul, and with all your mind. This is the first and greatest commandment. And a second is like it: You shall love your neighbor as yourself. Everything in the Law and the prophets hangs on these two commandments."

Usually, often through ignorance, we fail to grasp the full significance of these sentences. The practice of summarizing the Law in these two commandments and even that of comparing the second to the first is not specific to Jesus; it was also taught by his contemporaries. "You shall love your neighbor as yourself" is a summary of the Law found explicitly in the rabbinical writings of the period.[8]

The two commandments play a similar role here. Jesus takes two sentences to summarize the two Tables: the *Shema Israel* for the first commandments, and "you shall love your neighbor as yourself" from Leviticus for the second. Previously, in the text concerning the rich young man, I translated the "and," in "and you shall love your neighbor as yourself," by "in short" in order to show that it is not a matter of adding one commandment to another, but that what follows "and" is actually a usual summary. This was the way the commandments concerning the neighbor were evoked. There were commandments regarding God and commandments regarding the neighbor. Jesus summarized

8. The rabbi Aqiba (A.D. 45-135) said: "Love your neighbor as yourself, this is the great principle of the Torah."

the totality of the commandments in two sentences from Scripture. His response might be paraphrased as follows: "There is no one commandment that is greater than the rest. The greatest commandment is their totality." It is not a matter of choosing among them. He refers those who tempt him to the totality of God's Law, which is single and holy. No one commandment can be substituted for another. When Saint John says: "A new commandment I give to you, that you love one another, even as I have loved you" (John 13:34), the novelty lies in the words "as I have loved you." The point made is not with respect to the Law, but to the fulfillment of the Law, its interpretation, the way Jesus fulfills the commandments in yielding up his life.

The new commandment is the historical, concrete realization of all God's commandments through Jesus, the obedient Son. The way in which he fulfills the Law through complete and loving obedience to the Father reveals the Law in its perfection.

The commandment to love as Jesus loves is not to be substituted for the other commandments. That would make no sense. There is only one holy Law. The Law is the revelation of God's commandments. The newness is in God's act, in that he sends Israel his obedient Son. When, on the day of Pentecost, the Holy Spirit is poured out upon those who become Christ's brothers and sisters, that which the prophets promised is realized. Thus, God creates a people whose heart is born from the Holy Spirit and who, in the Spirit, will fulfill the commandments of holiness to perfection.

Here again — and Jesus tells us so — these two commandments sum up the entire Law as well as the prophets.

How does Jesus himself observe and fulfill these commandments? This is the crucial question: can we go deeper in our understanding of their role in Jesus' life and in that of his disciples?

The New Covenant

Jesus obviously spent much time meditating on the commandments. Everything Psalm 119 has to say about the "delights" of the Law was certainly an essential part of his prayer. We have proof of this in the Gospels' accounts of the principal events of his life, such as the temptations and his Passion. The commandments were constantly being meditated by Jesus as a word of life. Saint Matthew points out that during the temptation in the wilderness, Jesus cites Deuteronomy (8:3; 6:13, 16), referring explicitly to the *Shema Israel* — that is, to the observance of the commandments. In chapter 23, the maledictions regarding the Pharisees respond to the beatitudes of the Sermon on the Mount. These blessings and maledictions of the New Covenant, as it was promised by Jeremiah and Ezekiel, provide a framework for both a meditation on the Law and for its fulfillment: one of the key points of Jesus' life and preaching is to be understood through these two commandments, which sum up and imply all the rest.[9]

Now, let us return to the rich young man. The disciples are amazed and profoundly shaken by Jesus' demands. It seems to them that such a requirement would be impossible to meet: "Who then can be saved?" But Jesus' answer — and he looks directly at them as he gives it — is: "To men this is impossible; but to God all things are possible." This response is an explicit reference to the prophetic promise: since Israel has learned that it is not within man's power to remain faithful to the observance of the commandments, God's love goes so far as to promise to change man's heart and, in a freely bestowed gift, to enable him to keep his commandments.

The Covenant is the gift of the Law as a gift of life. The choice proposed to Israel is a choice between death and life. By observing the Covenant, Israel chooses life. If God is to reveal his grace and save all mankind, a decisive spiritual experience is required. Israel must feel its weakness, and discover that man cannot, by his own strength, preserve this gift of life; the weight of death in his existence is too great. Israel must recognize its utter weakness, its sin, to the point where it begs God for the strength to accomplish that which God asks of it. Therefore, the promise of the New Covenant is this: that God will become the partner of the one with whom he makes a Covenant, since it

9. Cf. Jeremiah 31 and Ezekiel 34-37.

is God himself who bestows his Spirit in the heart of Israel his son, and it is God's strength that will enable Israel to observe the Law. God will remove his people's heart of stone and replace it with a heart of flesh. It will no longer be only a broken and contrite heart (Psalm 51:19), a heart broken and crushed as a stone is crushed — but a living heart, filled with the Holy Spirit, one that can enter into a loving communion with God. These promises given in Deuteronomy are the New Covenant. The New Testament is nothing other than Deuteronomy, with the sole difference that what is given as a promise in Deuteronomy, is revealed by Jesus to be already fulfilled. What exactly does "fulfilled" signify? Just how great is the depth of God's love? How can God give a heart of flesh to man who does his will? How can God thus make Israel his faithful bride? This is the mystery revealed to us in Jesus the Christ, a mystery of immeasurable depth.

Why do these commandments have such importance? How can we increase our understanding of them?

The words from Leviticus — "You shall be holy; for I am holy" (11:44; 19:2) — are echoed in the Sermon on the Mount: "You, therefore, must be perfect, as your heavenly Father is perfect" (Matthew 5:48). It makes no sense to understand the Sermon on the Mount as the substitution of one commandment for another: "It was said to you; I say to you. . . ." One interpretation is being opposed to another, rather than one law being substituted for another. It is essential to understand what is meant by the expression "a new law."[10] If the novelty meant is that the Holy Spirit enters the heart of one who participates in Christ's life — the "law of the Spirit," as Saint Paul expresses it — then, yes, the expression "new law" is appropriate.[11] However, to maintain that revelation has been substituted for another is to understand absolutely nothing of the mystery of Christ. It is to deny the gift of God.

Why have these commandments been given to us?

10. The expression is not biblical. It appears much later in the Church's tradition and signifies the gift of the Holy Spirit, which makes it possible to live according to the grace of Christ and in conformity with his Gospel.

11. Cf. Romans 8:2 (literally): "the law of the Spirit of life."

If we are required to be perfect as our Heavenly Father is perfect, to be holy because God is holy, Jesus himself delivers the key to understanding this interpretation when, in the Sermon on the Mount, he invites us to forgive, to go beyond the law of "an eye for an eye . . .": "So that you may be sons of your Father who is in heaven, for he makes his sun rise on the evil and on the good" (Matthew 5:45). The Law enables us to act as God acts. And in Jesus' meditation, the Law reveals how God acts. Just as much as the Law is a precept given to man, it is also revelation of God's action and his mystery.

Such an interpretation may appear paradoxical because, we ask ourselves, how can "You shall not steal, shall not make graven images," etc. reveal God's activity and mystery? How can all these "orders," learned by rote in catechism, often regarded as slightly ridiculous or narrow-minded, be presented as the revelation of God's mystery? How can it be suggested that by observing the Ten Commandments, we act as God does, unless the commandments reveal to us how God acts?

We have to enter into Jesus' prayer — the Gospel makes it possible — to understand what the commandments tell us about the way God acts, how they allow us to participate in God's own action.

The common interpretation of the response to the rich young man, distinguishing the commandments from the counsels, does not go deep enough. The counsels, in this midrash, are part of the Law. They are, in fact, the first commandments, which shed light on all the others. Undoubtedly, there are several ways of observing certain precepts and practices in religious life: that of the Church of Jerusalem, as described in the Acts of the Apostles in the first days of Christianity, a community composed of observant Jews; an example of this way today is monastic life — whereas the Pagan-Christian communities do not have the same obligations. All, however, being ordered by love, which is the greatest good of the Church. This diversity is given for the edification of all; but there is only one way to observe the will of God and that is to obey the commandments.

The commandments themselves reveal something of the way God acts. For example, Jesus cites the commandment, "You shall not kill," including in it anger, insult, and then the necessity of reconciliation (cf. Matthew 5:21-26). Christ counters mankind's homicidal tendency with God's infinite capacity for forgiveness and benevolence. This brings us back to the fundamental mystery: God is not the author of death, but the Father of life, the giver of life.[12] He grants life and he forgives, since death, as we understand it, is both physical and carnal, and also sin. Forgiveness is a resurrection of the dead. And God observes the commandment "You shall not kill" by giving life and by forgiving; by resurrecting the dead and by being merciful. It is by participating in God's prodigious generosity and mercy that the disciple observes the commandment, "You shall not kill."

12. Cf. Wisdom of Solomon 1:13.

First Table

1. I am the Lord your God, who brought you out of the land of Egypt, out of the house of bondage.

2. You shall have no other gods before me. You shall not make for yourself a graven image, or any likeness of anything that is in heaven above, or that is in the earth beneath, or that is in the water under the earth; you shall not bow down to them or serve them; for I the Lord your God am a jealous God, visiting the iniquity of the fathers upon the children to the third and the fourth generation of those who hate me, but showing steadfast love to thousands of those who love me and keep my commandments.

3. You shall not take the name of the Lord your God in vain; for the Lord will not hold him guiltless who takes his name in vain.

4. Remember the sabbath day, to keep it holy. Six days you shall labor, and do all your work; but the seventh day is a sabbath to the Lord your God; in it you shall not do any work, you, or your son, or your daughter, your manservant, or your maidservant, or your cattle, or the sojourner who is within your gates; for in six days the Lord made heaven and earth, the sea, and all that is in them, and rested on the seventh day; therefore the Lord blessed the sabbath day and hallowed it.

5. Honor your father and your mother, that your days may be long in the land which the Lord your God gives you.

Second Table

6. You shall not kill.

7. You shall not commit adultery.

8. You shall not steal.

9. You shall not bear false witness against your neighbor.

10. You shall not covet your neighbor's house, you shall not covet your neighbor's wife, or his manservant, or his maidservant, or his ox, or his ass, or anything that is your neighbor's.

CHAPTER 2

The Ten Words

The Ten Commandments do not represent the totality of the Law, of its precepts, the *mitzvoth*. The idea that the Law can be summarized in different ways is seen frequently in Judaism. At least four or five summaries of the Law are proposed in the New Testament as well as in the contemporary rabbinical commentaries:

- The Ten Commandments, the ten words (Exodus 20:1-17).
- The *Shema Israel*: "Hear, O Israel: the LORD our God is one LORD" (Deuteronomy 6:4).
- The verse of Leviticus: "You shall love your neighbor as yourself" (Leviticus 19:18).
- "But the righteous shall live by his faith" (Habakkuk 2:4), quoted by Saint Paul (Romans 1:17), but which did not originate with him, nor with the Letter to the Hebrews.
- The summary that Jesus makes his own in the Sermon on the Mount (Matthew 7:12): "So whatever you wish that men would do to you, do so to them, for this is the law and the prophets." The same phrase is addressed by Hillel to a pagan, but formulated in the negative: "Whatever is detestable for you, do not do to your neighbor" (Shabbath 31 a).[1]

1. Hillel is certainly the most remarkable figure in the Pharisaic movement. He

The custom of summarizing the Law by various precepts is a spiritual practice that can also be found in the words of Saint Francis of Assisi: "All discipleship of Christ can be summed up in poverty." Such condensations consist of grasping a central aspect of the union with God and expressing it by a striking phrase whose role will be to concentrate spiritual energy. But such phrases do not claim to say everything nor exclude the rest.

The ten words which are the object of our meditation are one of the means proposed by Jesus to summarize the Law, means which he borrows from rabbinical tradition. As we meditate on them, we enter into the way in which he prayed, meditated, and received this teaching, and transmits it to us. We enter into the spiritual intuition at the heart of Christ's message; but this does not cover the totality of the commandments.

Let us try to see what these ten words reveal to us of the mystery of God, as well as what Jesus says to us and how the Messiah himself fulfills them.

Facing such questions, we can hardly find the words to speak. But we must dare to ask them since it is Christ himself — God himself — who invites us to do so. Asking ourselves these questions does not imply that we have the answers. We know that we are facing an inexhaustible, overwhelming mystery, in which God's splendor is revealed.

I shall only discuss a few of the commandments. Afterwards, each can continue on his/her own. What God will reveal to each of us will surpass by far anything we can say to each other.

I shall address the commandments in the order in which they are cited by Jesus in his encounter with the rich young man. We shall then return to the first Table.

---

was born to a noble family in Babylon around 50 B.C., under the reign of King Herod, and died around A.D. 10. He went up to the Land of Israel to pursue his studies and led a Spartan life. It is said that a pagan came to him to be converted on the condition that Hillel teach him the Torah while he stood on one foot! Hillel succeeded by summarizing it as follows: "If an act is detestable for you, do not inflict it on your neighbor. That is all the Torah, the rest is only commentary. Now go and learn."

"You Shall Not Kill"

The first commandment cited ("You shall not kill, you shall not commit murder") was commented on by Jesus himself in the Sermon on the Mount (Matthew 5:21 and following), which, I remind you, is an interpretation of the Law contrasted with other interpretations. The words "You have heard that it was said . . ." and "I say to you" refer to these interpretations. Christ is not substituting one law for another. Hence, this is a commentary on other commentaries.

Elsewhere, Jesus says: "Think not that I have come to abolish the Law and the prophets; I have come not to abolish them but to fulfill them. For truly, I say to you, till heaven and earth pass away, not an iota, not a dot, will pass from the Law until all is accomplished" (Matthew 5:17-18). And when Jesus says to his disciples that they are the "light of the world" (Matthew 5:14), that signifies that the light of the world is Israel, to the extent that Israel observes the Law. And the Law is the light of God, given to men for their salvation. This same expression, which in Saint Matthew is used by Jesus to refer to his disciples, is, in the Gospel of Saint John, used in referring to himself: "I am the light of the world."[2] In this way the evangelist emphasizes that this perfect fulfillment of the Law is given only in Jesus. The disciples are his disciples only to the extent that they participate in the fulfillment of the Law by Jesus himself. Just as "the salt of the earth" alludes to a "covenant of salt" (one of the forms of covenant in the Old Testament[3]), the disciples are the sign of the New Covenant which God makes with his people for the salvation of all mankind. They are to be the guarantors of the Covenant and of God's faithfulness.

Jesus comments on the first commandment by telling us to act as his Father does: with mercy and forgiveness. In what way is our Heavenly Father, the Father of Jesus Christ, merciful? And, thus, how can we say that he respects the commandment not to kill?

In Saint John's Gospel we find these words spoken by Jesus: "The

2. Cf. John 8:12; 9:5; 11:9.
3. Cf. Leviticus 2:13; Numbers 18:19; 2 Chronicles 13:4-5; see also Matthew 5:13.

devil . . . was a murderer from the beginning" (John 8:44), whereas God never created death, and is the Father of life. Not only does he give life, but he forgives sin, and the forgiveness of sin is itself a resurrection of the dead. The homicidal tendency that inhabits men's hearts kills them spiritually. When God forgives them, he returns them to life, he raises them from the dead. Jesus shows his disciples how to fulfill this commandment: to be merciful as their Heavenly Father is merciful.

The commandment not to kill is fulfilled by Jesus in his Passion. He gives himself up to the power of death because he bears the sins of the world. He places himself in the hands of God, who gives life and raises the dead. The risen Jesus is the source of forgiveness, the source of the gift of the Holy Spirit by whom God gives life.

Just as, by Jesus' death, the Holy Spirit is poured out, given, a source of forgiveness and a source of life, a source of perfection and of obedience to God, so the disciples are called to fulfill the commandment "You shall not kill" by imitating God's mercy and forgiveness. When we act thus, in Christ, we act with God's own power, we act as our Father in heaven acts, as Jesus himself acts.

Forgiveness, in the strongest sense of the word, can come only from God. He alone can forgive, because he alone can create. Man cannot create, cannot resuscitate the dead, cannot forgive, because his sin is the source of his death. Man may forget his own sin, he may bury it in oblivion or indifference, he may harden himself to past suffering, but true forgiveness is a strictly divine act. And if Jesus asks his disciples to forgive, it is because Israel and the disciples are being called to act as God acts, that is, by God's strength alone. If we understand the Law thus, in its perfection, it may seem impossible to observe, inapplicable, surpassing human strength. Yet God himself tells us: "For this commandment which I command you this day is not too hard for you, neither is it far off. It is not in heaven. . . . But the word is very near you; it is in your mouth and in your heart, so that you can do it" (Deuteronomy 30:11-14). If we have even the slightest idea that, after all, it may be possible to succeed on our own, we are doomed to failure. Because that would be to act humanly — and as human beings we can never forgive as God forgives. If we were to imagine that we can, we would be hypocrites, or liars, or victims of illusion. It is possible to act divinely in this world only with God's strength. The disciple thus finds himself confronted with both the full observance of the Law and his own inability to observe it, his own sin. He then turns to the prayer addressed by the people of God to the Lord: "Give us a new heart. Create in me a heart which can observe your laws" (cf. Psalm 51).

The Commandment concerning Adultery

How can we say that God observes the law concerning adultery?

The holiness of marriage proposed to Israel is reinforced by the interpretations which Jesus twice gives to it in the synoptic Gospels.[4] Marriage is the sign and sacrament of God's Covenant with his people. God does not commit adultery in the sense that he remains absolutely faithful to his Covenant, even when the people, attracted by idols, become adulterous. Man is constantly betraying God's faithfulness, whereas God's own faithfulness to the people he has chosen is absolute. This is also what allows us to commit ourselves, to God and to man, because the commitment is not based on our own faithfulness, but on that of God. Man's faithfulness in keeping this commandment and Israel's faithfulness are based on the fact that God himself is faithful. It is by experiencing its own unfaithfulness, its own adultery, that Israel can receive its true faithfulness from God. This is how Jesus himself sees it, when he presents himself as the Bridegroom of Israel: he is a sign and sacrament of the faithfulness of God who comes to inaugurate his reign and reclaim Israel, his bride, his faithful people.

This theme is found again in the Book of Revelation with the woman giving birth (Revelation 12:1-6). She is the bride who comes from heaven, that is, the Church.

How does Jesus himself fulfill this commandment? By presenting himself as the Bridegroom of the eschatological wedding. This is the

4. Cf. Matthew 19:1-9; 22:23-33.

significance of the wedding at Cana at which the wine of the eternal Kingdom is already inaugurated, anticipated by the coming of Jesus (John 2:1-12).

This wine of the eternal Kingdom is not the Eucharistic wine. In Saint Matthew's narrative of the Last Supper, Jesus says of the last cup: "Drink of it, all of you; for this is my blood of the covenant, which is poured out for many for the forgiveness of sins. I tell you I shall not drink again of this fruit of the vine until that day when I drink it new with you in my Father's kingdom" (Matthew 26:28-29). But the wine of the Kingdom referred to here is the wine of the final fulfillment. It is the wine which we shall drink with the Lord at the resurrection, and the wine of our Eucharist is only its anticipation. The wine of the Eucharist is the cup of Christ's Passion, which he allows us to share. It is not yet the wine of the eschatological banquet of the Risen Christ, the wine of the Promised Land which we are yet to receive, there where all mankind will be assembled, where there will no longer be any tears or suffering. There, we shall be able to commune in the joy of the wedding feast and the presence of the Bridegroom among his people. This is the wine of the eschatological Kingdom announced by Jesus when he reveals himself as the Bridegroom at the wedding at Cana. This wedding, Saint John tells us, is the first of the signs where the disciples see Jesus' glory and believe in him.

God's faithfulness to his people is fulfilled and given in Jesus the Messiah. This fulfillment in no way signifies that Israel is rejected. That would be to say that God is unfaithful; that would make a lie of God's Word and the word of Christ himself. This is a certitude that is not marginal but central to the Christian faith.

We well know that a mystery of sin and infidelity has existed throughout all of human history. But Christ is precisely the guarantee that God is faithful. That the mystery of salvation is a mystery of setting aside, of reserving for the future, a mystery whose logic escapes us, a mystery of redemption in which our experience of hope is often a hidden one and our experience of glory only through the Passion — is another matter. As Christ's disciples, we should be all the more prepared for and sensitive to this mystery. But so, even more than others,

Jesus' disciples can never imagine God as unfaithful. It is inconceivable. It is blasphemous.

*   *   *

All the other commandments on the second Table are negative as well. In applying them to God, they are comprehensible only through a positive translation.

"You shall not steal." How can man take possession of the goods of this world when everything belongs to God, the unique Lord and sovereign of the world? Saying that man should not steal from his neighbor is also saying that that those goods which he has legitimately acquired for himself belong to God who has given them to him: they are thus at the disposition of all. It would be worthwhile to reexamine the manner in which Jesus behaves toward worldly goods and in which he invites his disciples to act.

Similarly, the commandment concerning the bearing of false witness raises the question of truth. It is not limited to abstaining from false oaths. Jesus himself comments on this commandment in the Sermon on the Mount (Matthew 5:33 and following): "Let what you say be simply 'Yes' or 'No'; anything more than this comes from evil." It is an attestation to God's truth. Saint Paul refers to this phrase when he says that Jesus was totally "yes," was totally "amen,"[5] was total faithfulness and total truth of God, not allowing for the introduction of any lie within him. We should draw the connection between this and the theme of the deceitful, hypocritical heart found in Scripture and quoted abundantly by Jesus.[6]

---

5. Cf. 2 Corinthians 1:19.

6. Cf. Jeremiah 9:2-8, 25; Psalms 12:3; 119:113; Sirach 1:28; 2:12; 5:9; 6:1; Proverbs 11:20 and Job 36:13. See also Isaiah 1:10-20; 29:13-14; Amos 5:14-15, 21-27; 8:4-8 and Psalm 26:4 ("hypocrite"). The psalmist also speaks of "lips of deceit" (Psalms 17:1; 120:2). For Matthew, see 6:2, 5-16; 15:7, 8-9; 22:18; 23:13.

"Honor Your Father and Your Mother"

Finally, to return to the first Table: "Honor your father and your mother." Is it simply a matter of filial piety, in the sense that we commonly understand it? What can this mean with respect to God? How can God be said to observe such a commandment?

Could it not be that this commandment reveals the mystery of Election? When God asks us to honor our fathers and mothers — that is, those who have passed on to us, their descendants, the revelation of God — that means, concretely, the entire history of the Election, of God's revelation as the God of Abraham, Isaac, and Jacob, the God of the patriarchs. This commandment regarding fathers and mothers is that referred to in Deuteronomy: "And these words which I command you this day shall be upon your heart; and you shall teach them diligently to your children" (Deuteronomy 6:6-7). Through the generations of humanity, the Election and God's faithfulness are inscribed in history. And the way in which God himself observes the commandment can be seen in his choice of the patriarchs, in his choice of Israel. By choosing his people to be a blessing for all mankind, God makes of the history of human generation a history of salvation. It is not a question of honoring one's parents for the sake of obedience, but because the history of mankind's generation is a sacred history in the love of God for humanity, from which he chose Israel, his servant, so that all nations, in Israel, can participate in the same blessing.

Christ fulfills this commandment not only by his obedience to Joseph and Mary. Far more, he opens the family to an eschatological dimension when he says: "Who is my mother, and who are my brothers? . . . For whoever does the will of my Father in heaven is my brother, and sister, and mother" (Matthew 12:48, 50). He creates us as brothers in God, directing our obedience toward the only Father, the Heavenly Father.

"Remember the Sabbath Day"

Let us now look at the other commandments of the first Table, and first of all that which might appear the most surprising, the question of the Sabbath. Everything depends on the way the polemics surrounding the subject — found particularly in the synoptic Gospels — are understood. Modern readers tend to interpret them as describing an extremely formalistic, finicky, strict and ritualistic religion, as opposed to a broad-minded approach, opposed to clerical constraints and rigidities, with the aim of liberating the human condition. But according to the latter attitude, progress in the observance of the Law of God would consist of no longer observing anything and, consequently, of no longer respecting anything, since there would be no strict laws to be respected.

What, exactly, is at stake in the debate on the Sabbath as it is found in the synoptic Gospels? The meaning is striking when looked at closely. It is not a question of abolishing the observance of the Sabbath, but on the contrary, of giving it its full richness, its full accomplishment. Jesus presents himself as "Lord of the Sabbath." This is the precise and literal translation: "For the Son of man is lord of the sabbath" (Matthew 12:8). The Lord of the Sabbath is neither a tyrant nor someone who would abolish it; he fulfills it because he observes it. But just how does he observe it? As God himself observes it, who on the seventh day, rested and delighted in his creation.[7] The seventh day is the day on which God gives life and delights in man whom he has created, inviting him to enter into God's own life through the commandment to rest with him, to share in his joy in the Creation.

The Sabbath is the day when God's work of creation is completed, the day when his creature communes with the Creator's rest and joy, and acknowledges God as the Creator of all things. Jesus, who presents himself as the Lord of the Sabbath, comes to announce the eschatological Sabbath. On that day, he gives life, he heals. This question does not concern the details of what can or cannot be done on the Sabbath. What is really at stake centers on the person of Jesus. Jesus ob-

---

7. Cf. Genesis 2:2-3; Exodus 20:11; 31:17. See Hebrews 4:4, 5.

serves the Sabbath and announces the coming of the final Sabbath when the life of God is given in fullness to his people. Jesus, the "Lord of the Sabbath," he whom God sent, can give life and forgive sins on that day. If we were only dealing with casuistry over what is allowed and forbidden on the Sabbath, there would have been many defenders of his position among the rabbis of the time, even among the strictest.

Therefore, we as Christians must understand that we have entered into the first day of the eschatological week, which is Sunday. This is according to the Jewish way of counting the days, based on the days of creation, and also found in the narrative of the Resurrection.[8] In this first day of the week, the eschatological Shabbat is revealed. The joy of the disciples of Christ is to live in a kind of perpetual Sabbath. This leaves aside the problem of the practices and various traditions of the churches.

In any case, we can only understand the miracles performed by Jesus on the Sabbath and the polemic which they provoked if we understand the meaning of these actions, and what is at stake.

"I Am the Lord Your God"

Finally, let us look at the beginning of the Decalogue: "I am the LORD your God, who brought you out of the land of Egypt, out of the house of bondage. You shall have no other gods before me. You shall not make for yourself a graven image, or any likeness of anything that is in heaven above, or that is in the earth beneath, or that is in the water under the earth; you shall not bow down to them or serve them; for I the LORD your God am a jealous God, visiting the iniquity of the fathers upon the children to the third and the fourth generation of those who hate me, but showing steadfast love to thousands of those who love me and keep my commandments. You shall not take the name of the LORD your God in vain; for the LORD will not hold him guiltless who takes his name in vain."

---

8. Cf. Genesis 1:5; Matthew 28:1; Mark 16:2, 9; Luke 24:1; John 20:1, 19.

To understand these commandments, I propose that we return to the temptations of Jesus (Matthew 4:1-11), because this episode in the wilderness occurs just after Jesus has received the Spirit. From that moment, it is made clear that Jesus is able to fulfill the Law of God completely and perfectly, and so he acts as the true Israel should act, Israel promised by God, created by God. Therefore, his encounter with the Tempter in the desert, just as Israel was tested on coming out of Egypt, will focus on God and on the totality of his Law.

The first temptation is to give oneself life rather than receive it from God alone. Jesus answers with a quotation: "Man does not live by bread alone, but . . . by everything that proceeds out of the mouth of the LORD" (Deuteronomy 8:3).

The second temptation is of the same order. The Devil says to Jesus, "If you are the Son of God" — hence, as in the first temptation, "if you are faithful and true Israel" — "throw yourself down from the top of the pinnacle." The Devil places Jesus above the Holy of Holies, and tells him, "Throw yourself down," quoting Psalm 91: "For he will give his angels charge of you. . . . On their hands they will bear you up, lest you dash your foot against a stone." Jesus replies, "You shall not put the LORD your God to the test" (Deuteronomy 6:16). In other words, an act of faith has no meaning other than the service of God, rather than appropriating God's promise for ourselves. To believe in God's promise is to do only what God wishes, and to do this solely to glorify God, the Unique and Good, not to reap benefit for oneself.

You remember the third temptation: "The devil took him to a very high mountain, and showed him all the kingdoms of the world and the glory of them; and he said to him, 'All these I will give you, if you will fall down and worship me.' Then Jesus said to him, 'Begone, Satan! for it is written, "You shall worship the Lord your God and him only shall you serve."'" (Matthew 4:8-10) We are to worship the unique God who reveals himself as the source of life. He is a living God, whereas idols are dead. In giving us his Word, he reveals the meaning of his creation and of our existence. In his Word made flesh, his obedient Son makes it possible for us to fulfill his commandments.

These temptations, with which Satan tempts Christ in the desert,

28

refer us to the Passion, where the same challenge is addressed to Christ on the Cross: "If you are the Son of God . . ." (Matthew 27:40).

We see clearly how Jesus, at the very moment of the Passion, fulfills the commandments and precepts of the Law. God keeps his word by giving life to his obedient Son: he raises him from the dead. And in Jesus, the obedient Son, the believer receives proof that God is faithful and gives life to those who trust in him. The fact that he does not allow his Righteous One to see corruption[9] is proof that the Law is indeed the source of life. Since Jesus is resurrected from the dead and not locked up in *Sheol*, we have proof that death has no hold on him. If God has resurrected him from the dead, it means that the divine Law is indeed the source of life and that it gives us life through and in Christ.

The good news announced by Jesus is that he is himself this Good News, the Kingdom at hand. The Kingdom which has drawn near to us is none other than Christ himself.

We must reflect again and again, as we penetrate more deeply, on the grace we have received in having been baptized in Christ, and, thus, of sharing in his condition. We must reflect, and try to approach as best we can, this mystery of the Kingdom which is Christ himself: a hidden, buried mystery, a mystery of dereliction and suffering. A mystery which remains incomprehensible in a time already belonging to the last days, the days of God's Day, when the mystery of God works, and yet the mystery of iniquity seems still to reign and does in fact reign until the end of time when all things are achieved and God will be "all, and in all."[10]

The reign of God is given to us in Christ in a hidden manner, as he himself tells us:[11] it is not elsewhere, not here or there, not before or after.[12] It is to be received from the mystery of Christ himself, who se-

---

9. "Righteous One" is a Christological title used throughout the New Testament: cf. Acts of the Apostles 3:14; 7:52; 22:14; 1 John 2:1, 29; 3:7; Revelation 16:5. The title undoubtedly evokes the "suffering servant" in the Old Testament; cf. Isaiah 53:11. Psalm 16:10 is quoted in the Acts of the Apostles 2:27, regarding the resurrected Christ.

10. Cf. Colossians 3:11.

11. Cf. Matthew 13:44.

12. Cf. Matthew 24:23.

cretly communicates himself to his disciples so that they can participate in the holy mission to which they are called by the Father's will.
Just as Christ is given to the Father and is given to us, we are given to
Christ to be with him, as Saint John says (Mark 13:13-14), and to participate in his action and in his work. Thus, we shall share in the mystery
of Israel, the mystery of Election, and the mystery of love as it is given
and desired by God for the salvation of the whole world — but in
Christ, at the heart of the mystery of redemption, which is a mystery of
contradiction. By this very fact, it is given to us to be the depositaries
and guarantors of Hope.

CHAPTER 3

Prophecy concerning the Life of Jesus

L et us turn now to the second chapter of Saint Matthew, which gives an account of the Adoration of the Wise Men, the Flight to Egypt, the Massacre of the Innocents, and the Return of the Holy Family. The liturgy turns each event into a separate feast, whereas the chapter forms a whole, in which each event is unintelligible on its own. We shall concentrate on the entire mystery of Christ, as it is presented in these first chapters — which are as much a *Midrash* as an apocalypse.

Rather than give a complete and detailed explanation of this chapter, I should like to point out certain aspects. In fact, by using a hieratic form, the author emphasizes the prophetic force of even the smallest details. In this one chapter, the entire mystery of Christ is being presented to us.

Entering into a Singular History and Remembering It

If the evangelist takes the trouble to begin his narrative with a genealogy, it indicates that he is not describing just any child, from just any background. This child is the one who is revealed as a sign, as the hope of the Gentile nations, and as the salvation of all. He is this child and no other, the one whose particular history we must accept; for otherwise, without the history preceding his birth, there can be no Savior of all mankind. The path the pagans must take is precisely the one leading to Jerusalem, to welcome this specific Messiah in this specific history. Going even further, just as there is no history without Election by God, so too the pagans can only enter into the history of salvation and be saved if they make this history their own.

Election is the revelation of a choice made by God. This choice is not arbitrary like human choices. Man cannot choose, he can only oscillate; he can choose only to the extent that he is truly free. When God chooses, however, it is a creative act of love in order to teach men that they are loved by God and can love with God's own love. When God chooses, he creates, he calls; and God's choice provides man with an absolute reference for his own history. Election begins with God's first gesture toward man, when he says: "Let us make man, Adam, in our image." Man's creation, through God's revelation of that creative act, emerges from the obscurity of the cosmos to become a history which is a personal relationship with God and which opens a future to man. There is history only because of God's choice: there was a day on which God called his servant Abraham, when he called his people from Egypt. . . . There is true history only in accordance with an Election, because history is, ultimately, a time period which draws its significance from a relationship with God who calls and toward whom we go. Otherwise, all human acts sink into the insignificance of oblivion and death. Otherwise, no memory is possible — it is even better to forget. Otherwise, human history is an abyss of meaninglessness and horror and the moments of light are merely faint sparks marked, too, by oblivion and death. Only God can be the source of man's memory. Only God can make of human history a source of blessing, because God alone can enable those he has chosen to remember. This explains why Israel is entrusted with the world's memory, why Christ is the world's memory, and why thus the Christians are responsible for preserving this memory. In them alone does the world find its meaning, even if the secret is well hidden. The only history which has a meaning is that which we recall in the Eucharist, Christ's Memorial.

It is into this particular history of Election that we must enter.

The pagans themselves only participate in salvation if they enter into this history, and if the grace is given to them that it become their own history. Thus, Isaiah's words — "For to us a child is born, to us a son is given" (Isaiah 9:6) — become words that Christ's disciple in the Church can repeat with Israel. He receives the grace that Israel's history becomes his own history, and he too can say: "Our father Abraham."[1]

In the announcement to Joseph, Saint Matthew presents Jesus as the Emmanuel, that is, he who is completely filled by the Holy Spirit, born from the force of the Holy Spirit, Son of God in a sense that is yet entirely implicit; the language is that of revelation. This Emmanuel, born of God, will accomplish in full the vocation of Israel, as expressed by Saint John, who receives these words from Jesus: "My food is to do the will of him who sent me" (John 4:34). These words echo those found in the Old Testament: "Man does not live by bread alone, but . . . by everything that proceeds out of the mouth of the LORD" (Deuteronomy 8:3). Food for the man in whom the Spirit dwells is to accomplish the Father's holy will; to rejoice and to let his hunger be satisfied by God's gift, in the freedom of the Spirit.

This is Israel's vocation; this is the vocation of the Messiah.

The Sin of Herod, the Pagan King: His Refusal of Israel's Election . . .

The first point I will make about chapter 2 is that here, for the moment, we are only dealing with Israel and the pagans; and most often we fail to see clearly who is Israel and who are the pagans.

The most common reading of this chapter assimilates Herod to Israel and sees Jesus only as Jesus himself. Whereas, in fact, the entire logic of the narrative is directed toward showing that Israel is Jesus and that Herod is not the king of Israel. Herod is a pagan, an Idumean,[2] one

---

1. Cf. Genesis 17:4, 5; Romans 4:12, 16, 17.

2. Idumea was a country which included southern Judea and a northern section of Arabia. The Idumeans, also called Edomites, were the descendents of Esau, surnamed Edom. Cf. Genesis 25:30; 27:33-41; 36:1-8; 1 Chronicles 1–3; 1 Maccabees 5:3.

of the usurper kings who ruled Israel. He is not a descendant of David, nor is he a high priest; he does not incarnate Israel's hope, even if he satisfies certain nationalist aspirations, even if he rebuilt the Temple.

Jesus, the Messiah, answers Israel's hope, while Herod, the king, represents nothing more than a form of pagan power. Herod-the-king's behavior, to a certain extent, parallels that of Pilate, the governor, during the Passion. This second chapter of Saint Matthew's Gospel is already a prophecy of Jesus' Passion, and Herod plays the role that will later be that of Pilate the pagan.

Here, Israel is represented by the child and by Joseph. The pagans are represented both by Herod and by the three wise men. The people of Israel is not named as a people; there are only the chief priests and scribes who appear as witnesses, in a role limited to providing the key, the interpretation, of the story, and who allow the story to unfold and find its meaning.

The first point we note is that the evangelist shows us how the appearance of the child, of the promised Messiah, immediately arouses the radical hostility of the kings of this world and provokes a mortal conflict. (It should be noted that, contrary to popular traditions, the three wise men are not kings.) By his reaction to the appearance of the King-Messiah, the enemy unmasks himself, and in the figure of Herod the enemy is revealed as that which he truly is: a deathly power.

It is important to understand clearly both the figure of Herod, and his sin. His sin — the evangelist tells us — is his refusal to recognize that which is given as "good news," the grace bestowed on Israel. He refuses Israel's Election in order to claim it for himself, to set himself up in place of Israel. The king given by God is his enemy since Herod has made himself king and usurped God's place with his people. Herod, who has anointed himself or been named by the pagan authorities, is bound to reject and kill the king of Israel given by God. Herod's sin, the pagans' sin, is to refuse the Election because it appears to them as a mortal threat: it overturns all power in this world by showing that the sole master and Lord of this world is God himself. Israel's vocation is to attest to this truth, and Jesus gives its supreme attestation.

. . . to the Point of Murder

Herod's sin is not only to refuse the King-Messiah, but to pursue this refusal to the point of massacre. How will this refusal be carried out?

The evangelist gives us a staggering, almost unbearable account of these events: the refusal of the Messiah, who is prophetically put to death by Herod — before the act is carried out by the Romans — through the massacre of the children of the line of David. The children are massacred uniquely because they are descendants of the House of David.

After the lessons of history, how could such a text not be unbearable? We are seized with vertigo in the face of such prophetic depth. We hardly dare to advance further, as if it would be a blasphemy to dare to think that God could permit such horror for his people, for his beloved Son.[3]

But this is precisely what the evangelist tells us: the refusal of the Election and the Messiah means that Herod murders the descendants of David and all the children of Bethlehem. The biblical precedent is known to us: Pharaoh, too, commanded the midwives of Israel to kill all the male children, and Moses was a survivor of that massacre.[4]

The "Scandal" of Rachel: The Night of Faith

The biblical reference is clear. The way in which the evangelist quotes Jeremiah (31:15) is also remarkable: "A voice was heard in Ramah, wailing and loud lamentation, Rachel weeping for her children; she refused to be consoled, because they were no more" (Matthew 2:18). In Jeremiah, the verse which follows reads: "Thus says the LORD: 'Keep your voice from weeping, and your eyes from tears; for your work shall be rewarded,' says the LORD, 'and they shall come back from the land of

---

3. The people of Israel are the "dear son of God" (see, for example, Jeremiah 31:20).

4. Cf. Exodus 1:16-22.

the enemy. There is hope for your future,' says the LORD, 'and your children shall come back to their own country. I have heard Ephraim bemoaning'" (Jeremiah 31:16-18).

Saint Matthew quotes only verse 15, in order to emphasize Rachel's absolute despair, which seems to refuse the "Comforter" — one of the names for the Messiah. If Rachel refuses the Comforter, it is because of the pagans' sin. Her suffering is too great. She conceals even her hope, and cannot recognize, in the massacre of her sons whom she mourns, the hope of the Comforter which is nevertheless present.

This should lead us to reflect on the pagans' sin regarding Israel's Election and regarding Christ. How can we not think of Jesus' words: "Whoever causes one of these little ones who believe in me to sin, it would be better for him to have a great millstone fastened round his neck and to be drowned in the depth of the sea" (Matthew 18:6)?

These are terrible words — words of striking violence — coming from the mouth of Jesus. It is the little ones who are scandalized. For the real scandal is to stumble in our faith, to cease to believe in God when faced with the horror of evil. It is to falter in our hope in God or of the Messiah. This is the meaning of scandal, not the hypocritical indignation of the self-righteous or the contradiction of received wisdom. Scandal is to stumble in our faithfulness to God. It is exactly what Jesus experiences when, facing his Passion, he says to Peter, "Get behind me, Satan! You are a hindrance to me" (Matthew 16:23). Rachel's scandal is of the same kind: it is that she dares not believe, facing death and the ordeal of loss, that God is the source of life. It is not daring to trust in God.

In reading Elie Wiesel's *The Night*, written, at the urging of François Mauriac, years after his return from the concentration camps — and, until then, he had been unable to speak about the experience — we can ask ourselves whether the pagans of the twentieth century have not committed this sin referred to by Jesus, that of scandalizing the little ones, who thus stumbled in their faith and ceased to believe in God's goodness.[5] Wiesel writes that, on arriving at the camp as the

5. Elie Wiesel, born in Hungary in 1928, was deported to Auschwitz. His first work, *La Nuit (The Night)*, for which Mauriac wrote the Preface, was published in France

only survivor of the massacre carried out in his village, he cried to himself, "Never shall I forget those moments which murdered my God and my soul. . . . Never shall I forget these things, even if I am condemned to live as long as God Himself." And he evokes "the day, horrible even among those days of horror" when Wiesel, a child, "watched the hanging (yes!) of another child who . . . had the face of a sad angel, and he heard someone behind him groan, 'Where is God? Where is He? Where can He be now?' And a voice within answered: 'Where? Here He is — He has been hanged here, on these gallows.'"[6] At that moment, night fell on Wiesel's faith in God, because God henceforth appeared to him to be absent.

Similarly, Herod's sin is that Rachel does not wish to be consoled, and that the world must wait for her to be consoled. How long must we wait before she accepts the Comforter and consolation? The sin of the pagans, too, will have to be forgiven by the Messiah, and by him alone, for he alone can say: "Father, forgive them; for they know not what they do."[7] Jesus says this of the pagans who kill the innocent, who cause the faithful to stumble in their faith. His words retain an historic and concrete meaning; yet this sin, of the massacre of the innocents, will also require forgiveness, but it can be forgiven only by the Messiah of Israel and by no one else.

Thus, Herod's sin is the refusal of Israel's Election, and his sin is revealed as a source of death.

The Wise Men: The Adoration of the Pagans and the Murderous Plans of Herod

What provokes Herod's conduct? It is here that the coming of the Wise Men, a different figure of the pagans, is extraordinary. They are the

---

in 1958. He received the Médicis Prize for *Le Mendiant de Jérusalem* (*The Beggar of Jerusalem*) in 1960 and was awarded the Nobel Peace Prize in 1986.

6. François Mauriac, Préface to *La Nuit* (Paris: Editions de Minuit, 1958), p. 13. Translation given according to the English edition, MacGibbon and Kee, 1960, pp. 9-10.

7. Cf. Luke 23:34.

sign, the protagonists, the anticipated and prophetic realization of those who, not yet knowing God, come nevertheless to submit themselves to the Anointed One of the Lord and to pay homage to him, as described by Isaiah (chapter 61) or Psalm 72: the pagans will come to worship the Lord and recognize his Messiah.

The arrival of the Wise Men provokes the Messiah's death; Herod hears the Wise Men's news and decides to kill the child of Bethlehem. There is here a direct link — mysterious and incomprehensible for human logic — which is specific to the message of the New Testament. It is the link between the pagans' entry into the promise given to Israel and the putting to death of the Messiah and his Resurrection. The Messiah can fulfill his role only by being put to death by that which he has come to accomplish. He is put to death because of the pagans and for the pagans, as well as for Israel. It is at the price of his death that he can open the Covenant of Israel to the pagans. The pagans are both the beneficiaries of this turnabout and the very ones who provoke the Passion of the Messiah of Israel.

Jesus, the Child of Bethlehem, "Set Apart" . . .

The evangelist presents Jesus as one of the children of Bethlehem. He is, according to the words of Isaiah, the one who is "set apart," placed in reserve, the *Netzer*. There is a difficult play on words here. It seems that the word *Nazarene* should be related to the word *Netzer*, which is found several times in Isaiah, in particular in the poem of the Servant (Isaiah 60:21): he is the "shoot," or offspring, that is set aside, placed in reserve by God, in order to accomplish Israel's redemption. Jesus is spared not because of the children, but rather reserved, spared from their massacre to accomplish, obediently and by a sovereign and voluntary act, that which the children endure as an incomprehensible suffering. He is the one who shares Israel's exodus and exile, flees to Egypt and returns, and in so doing anticipates the mystery of his Passion. At the end of his Gospel, Saint Matthew shows us the accomplishment of the prophecies: on the Cross, Jesus is again designated by a pagan as the king of the Jews, and the pagans recognize him despite his Passion.

In this conflict, the figure shown to us of the Son and Messiah sums up the totality of Israel. It is a prophetic text in which the evangelist — as Isaiah and the prophets often do — plays with what the exegetes have called the "corporate personality," which refers to both a person and a people.[8] The figure of the Messiah is at the same time a figure of Israel; the figure of Jesus is at the same time that of his people, of his Church, and a figure of Israel. What is said of one can sometimes be applied to the other, sometimes to both. Many things can be understood only by recognizing this solidarity of Jesus with those who are his, of the Messiah with his people. Thus, at this prophetic moment, these seemingly distinct and opposing events are seen to anticipate the history of Jesus, the history of the Church. It is likely that the evangelist was unaware of how much he included in his history of salvation, since the full import of his words is revealed only after their fulfillment. It is normal that we too should discern here our own fulfillment, of which the author could not have been aware.

. . . to Be the Savior of All

In this prophetic vision, Jesus is both what he represents and what will be engendered in him. Jesus, the child, is both Israel and his people, the totality of his people. By that very fact, he is the Savior of all. We believe that in Jesus the totality of mankind, loved by God, receives, in hope, the gift which God wishes to give them. We believe that in Jesus is given for all, in hope, the communion of salvation and that all, in some way, are present in him and already receive, in him, the beginning of the accomplishment that God destines for all mankind.

This prophecy, rooted in history and itself a part of history, calls

---

8. The expression "corporate personality" was coined at the end of the nineteenth century by Anglo-Saxon exegetes. It designates a person who represents a people, for example, Adam represents humanity; Jacob, the people of Israel.

us to give thanks for the promise made to Israel and now open to all, for the gift of this child. It allows us, already, to measure the sin from which God wishes to deliver us. For the figure of Herod is not merely that of an enemy; he is already a witness to Christ's Passion, a sign of Christ's Passion, in whom man's sin is revealed. It is necessary that the Messiah be rejected, because the murderous instinct that dwells in human hearts must be exposed for God to heal man of his yearning for death and his homicidal tendencies. The Messiah is the one who takes upon himself this homicidal tendency in submitting himself to it and who, rather than turning it into death, transforms it into forgiveness.

For the true King of Israel will not govern his people like Herod; he will not replace Herod. The reign inaugurated by Jesus will be the absolute negation of Herod's, because the reign of Israel's Messiah, the reign of Jesus the King-Messiah, is exercised by the force of God, by forgiveness, truth, mercy, holiness, the capacity to deliver from sin and to resurrect the dead. In the figure of Herod, on the other hand, sin is revealed as homicidal and as a denial of God's grace.

In the massacre of the innocent children of Bethlehem, we can thus see — in a way which may be scandalous and terrifying for our sensibilities — the prophetic announcement of the nature of all sin, which is always a refusal of Election, a refusal of grace, a refusal of God, a compromise with the homicidal tendencies in man's heart. And in the death of these innocent children, as well as in God's providential actions, when he "sets apart" his Son and leads him through the path of the Exodus from Egypt — set apart to be given as hope when he returns to the land of Israel — we see the figure of all redemption.[9]

If we pray as we should, we cannot fail to recognize ourselves in each of the protagonists of this prophecy — sometimes in one, sometimes in another — because none of us can place himself solely in one camp or the other. All of us need to be redeemed. We must see our rejections and refusals, as they are revealed by God's grace. We must contemplate the grace given to us in having our sins forgiven and in that we too can recognize the King.

9. Cf. Matthew 2:15, 20, 21.

CHAPTER 4

Prophecy of the Life of the Disciples of Jesus

C hapter 2 of Saint Matthew's Gospel is a remarkable prophecy of both the life of Jesus and that of the Church. It is prophetic even in its most paradoxical aspects in that, in a way, the account of Jesus' later life will add nothing concerning his mission that has not already been announced here.

The sign of fulfillment is given to us: the pagans come to discover the Messiah of Israel. This Messiah remains unknown, hidden; he escapes death through God's power, thus fulfilling his Word. He is the sign and guarantee of the hope already being realized, yet he remains hidden, "set apart." The mystery of his being "placed in reserve," of his concealment and future revelation is suggested, and yet, the concealment remains complete.

In this prophecy, we can glimpse an announcement of the condition of Jesus' future disciples. They share in the Messiah's condition, in his suffering, and are concealed with him in this time of history in which they hope for the coming of the Son of Man, in glory, on the clouds of heaven. This is the time of the Church, a time of vigilant expectation.

This chapter sheds light on our personal condition and that of the Church. Let us try to see what spiritual lesson can be drawn. I invite you to compare it with the parables of judgment given by Jesus to his disciples at the end of his eschatological sermon.

These parables describe the time of history and, in teaching us how to live in anticipation of the fulfillment of that time, allow us to deepen our understanding of this second chapter.

The parables of judgment begin at verse 42 of chapter 24 and continue until the end of chapter 25. Saint Matthew has just reported the "eschatological" discourse, the discourse on the last days, that Jesus pronounces in the Temple, shortly before his Passion. It is followed by his words on the "day and the hour" which is unknown to all, even the Son. "But of that day and hour no one knows, not even the angels of heaven, nor the Son, but the Father only." Then Jesus announces the Second Coming, the *Parousia* of the "Son of Man." Next comes a series of parables describing the time when the "Son of Man" will be absent and the mystery of the judgment. This time of absence of the "Son of Man" is our time. Today the Messiah is hidden. Only Peter, James, and John have seen his glory in the company of Moses and Elijah. We live in hope of the coming of the Son of Man in his glory. Jesus' teaching, his ultimate instructions to his disciples, are for this time, the time of absence, in which his disciples must watch and wait, and for which Christ gives them the wisdom needed.

Saint Matthew begins with the three parables of "vigilant expectation." I quote them without commentary: the parable of the thief, that of the two servants — one wise, one foolish — and, finally, the parable of the ten virgins waiting for the return of the bridegroom. What is this oil with which the wise virgins fill their lamps? How is this oil necessary to watch through the night and, in spite of their sleepiness, to be ready to go in with the bridegroom to the marriage feast?

*   *   *

The three parables of vigilance are followed by two parables of judgment. First comes the judgment of the stewards of the kingdom, commonly known as the "Parable of the Talents." Who are the stewards? I believe they represent both Israel and the disciples of Christ, without a distinction being made between them by Saint Matthew. They represent those who have received God's riches in deposit.

The second parable is that of the judgment of the pagan nations. When the Son of Man comes in his glory, and all the angels with him, he sits on his throne and gathers before him all the pagan nation. It is the judgment of the pagans, who do not know the Messiah and who have not received the treasures of God's Election. Consequently, it is not the judgment of Christ's disciples, those who will be called "Christians" at Antioch, whether they come from among the Jews or the pagans;[1] and it is not the judgment of the Jewish people, who cannot be counted among the "nations" *(goyim)*.

The Judgment of the Servants of the Kingdom: Israel and the Church of Christ

Let us look in more detail at these two parables, and first of all the "Parable of the Talents," concerning the stewards of the kingdom. "For it will be as when a man going on a journey called his servants and entrusted to them his property" (Matthew 25:14).

It is very clear that the reference is to the master's own servants; that is, those whom God has chosen: Israel and Jesus' disciples. In this time of absence, God entrusts all his property to his own servants. The talents are obviously the treasures of God's grace, the treasures of his Kingdom. Any speculation on the reference to human gifts applies only insofar as they can be considered as a part of the treasures of God's grace. There exists a stoical and strictly humanistic interpretation of this parable which would make the text cry out in indignation if it were not stifled by the commentaries!

In fact, the master entrusts to each servant what he deems appropriate: five talents, two talents, and one talent, respectively. And the servant's mission is to manage the treasures of the kingdom according to the master's own logic, not to safeguard them like a deposit. The steward who buried the talent in the ground acted conscientiously, strictly observing the biblical law of deposits, which teaches that an

---

1. Cf. Acts of the Apostles 11:26.

entrusted deposit was to be kept with the greatest of care, preserved safely to be returned to the owner the day he asks for it.

But it is precisely this law of deposits that is challenged by the master, who refers to another exigence. The servant must act according to the revelation that has been made to him of who the master is and, hence, what he expects of him. The wicked servant passes judgment on himself by revealing the idea he has of God. And it is on this basis that God judges him, since God's riches have been entrusted to him to produce according to God's logic; that is, according to the logic of the generosity of giving, of the free gift of grace, and of the fruitfulness of God's word given to man. The servants, Israel and Christ's Church, are judged according to their faithfulness to the divine way of acting with regard to the gifts received, God's property.

The Judgment of the Pagan Nations:
Their Right to the Initial Benediction

Next comes the judgment of the pagans. It is on this in particular that I wish to pause, because the account of this judgment will enable us to return to the great parable of chapter 2. How is the judgment of the nations, of the Gentiles, presented?

We are dealing here, I repeat, with the judgment of the pagan nations. This is said explicitly: "When the Son of man comes in his glory, and all the angels with him, then he will sit on his glorious throne. Before him will be gathered all the nations (all the pagan nations), and he will separate them one from another as a shepherd separates the sheep from the goats, and he will place the sheep at his right hand, but the goats at the left." It is thus the Shepherd-King of Israel who comes. As Shepherd-King of Israel, he gathers before him all the pagan nations.

The chosen of Israel are not among the peoples being judged. They have been judged already; they are standing beside the judge. Jesus himself said this explicitly when he answered his disciples, "You who have followed me will also sit on twelve thrones."[2] We must try to understand the astonishing scene presented here.

The Shepherd-King first pronounces the same blessing on the nations he will place on his right as on Israel: "Come, blessed of my father." They are thus entitled to the same blessing as the brothers of the Messiah. They are entitled to the same blessing as the disciples on whom Jesus has pronounced the Beatitudes. They are entitled to the blessing given to the Church herself: "Inherit the kingdom prepared for you from the foundation of the world" (Matthew 25:34). They are thus entitled to the original blessing which God reserves, from the creation of the world, for those he has chosen.[3]

This means that, in the history of salvation, the Election is destined for all men when the hidden mystery shall be revealed, when the time of history shall be achieved, when that which is presently invisible and indistinguishable to the eyes of men — and is known only to those who share in Christ's faith — will at last be brought to light.

Hence, they too are entitled to this blessing, and to the Kingdom of God. "Then the King will say to those at his right hand, 'I was hungry and you gave me food, I was thirsty and you gave me drink, I was a stranger and you welcomed me, I was naked and you clothed me, I was sick and you visited me, I was in prison and you came to me.' Then the righteous will answer him, 'Lord, when did we see thee hungry and feed thee, or thirsty and give thee drink? And when did we see thee a stranger and welcome thee, or naked and clothe thee? And when did we see thee sick or in prison and visit thee?' And the King will answer them, 'Truly, I say to you, as you did it to one of the least of these my brethren, you did it to me.'"[4]

2. Cf. Matthew 19:28.
3. Cf. Ephesians 1:3-4.
4. Cf. Matthew 25:35-45.

The Disciples Who Live the Beatitudes to the Cross

The "least of those" to whom all this is done are those who share Christ's Passion because they have been called to do so by God's Election. They are those who, for the justice of the Kingdom, accept imprisonment, accept persecution for justice's sake; those who accept hunger and thirst as Jesus accepts hunger and thirst in his Passion, those who accept being stripped of all property as Jesus is stripped of his clothing, to be thrown into prison as he was, those who are willing to be, in this world, the sign and the members of the suffering and humiliated Messiah. They thus become, in this world, the instruments for the world's judgment, unknown even to those among whom they act.

They participate in the salvation of the world through their compassion with Christ as they share his Passion. They are, in the time of history, the means by which God permits all mankind to be judged and saved. In this time of Christ's concealment, they are called to be the presence of the suffering Christ-Messiah. They stand alongside Christ, judging the nations, because they have been members of Christ, suffering for and because of the nations.

Christ's reign is described here. This enumeration reminds us of the Beatitudes, because the final blessings that Jesus addresses to the pagans are essentially the counterparts of the blessings he addresses to the disciples who are going to share his Passion. The Beatitudes, in fact, are specifically addressed to those who participate in the Messiah's work in the New Covenant — to those who hunger and thirst for justice, for holiness, and who are persecuted because of this justice, thus sharing Christ's Passion. They are already the blessed. And in their suffering they become the instrument of the blessing which remains hidden and unknown to the very ones who benefit from it, until the final surprise where it will be revealed to both.

In our time, the time of history, the disciples know that they must continue to take their part in Christ's work, but the last judgment is not yet arrived, for them as for the rest. They too are still living in the obscure time of the Passion, of being "hidden away" with Christ. I believe there is a link to be made with Saint Paul's words to the Colossians: "Henceforth, your life is buried with Christ" (3:3), or buried *in* Christ.

And when Saint John says, "It does not yet appear what we shall be" (1 John 3:2), he is expressing fundamentally this same intuition of a time in which things remain hidden. Nevertheless, already they have been given and are attainable in the eyes of faith. The faithfulness of Jesus' disciples, of Christians — thus, of the members of Christ, the Messiah — is to share his faithfulness so as to accomplish the mission given to them. They are to labor until the end of time. They know that this duration in history is the time in which, by their perseverance, they work toward the salvation of mankind and the completion of the judgment which has already begun.

Bringing Forth the Light of the Messiah Buried in the Secret of History

Now we can return to chapter 2 of the Gospel according to Matthew, and to the light it sheds on the condition of the Church and the faithful. Let us try to receive this mystery of the unknown, unrecognized Messiah, buried in the secret of history, recognized by pagans, the Wise Men, who worship him and give him their presents perhaps without knowing who he is. This Messiah reveals the sin of the pagans, of Herod, by making himself their victim; he is thus the instrument of forgiveness through his Passion. God's power triumphs by saving him, by making the Messiah a survivor of death rather than allowing the destruction of the innocent. This is what we are as Christians. Not having escaped a sudden death, but united by God's power to death offered with Christ and, therefore, the first-fruits of the hope for all nations which remain under the power of death. The specific characteristic of pagans is to be those who do not know that darkness can be transformed into light, who do not know that they are sinners, that they can be forgiven and that death can be vanquished, by God alone, the source of life.

Our time is the time when darkness and death still reign, and when, nonetheless, we are charged with bringing forth the light.

Only in Christ can we find the courage to look at this mystery of the Passion and sin, as revealed in the massacre of the innocent, without trembling or running away, without succumbing to the despair that such a vision entails. We can bear this Passion of Christ as well as this passion of Israel in God's compassion, and so can pray both that sins be forgiven and that this Passion find its meaning. It is an immense secret, which can be shared only by those who are willing to carry the same burden. But we must not seek to console Rachel; we must pray for Rachel and for her children. The only way to do this is to be united with the compassion of that other Rachel, the one of whom Rachel is already a figure: the Virgin Mary who stands silently at the foot of the Cross, whose child has also been taken from her, but who lives in hope, the very sign of the compassionate Church, sharing both the Passion of her Lord and his silence.

Then our prayer can contain, always in secret, the hope of pardon for the executioners as well as the hope of life for those who succumb to them. That is our important and vital mission for the Church's faith and the salvation of the world.

CHAPTER 5

The Passion of Christ throughout History

W hat I am about to say now can be received only when standing before the Crucified Christ, before the Risen Christ showing us his wounds. It can be understood only in the very heart of the Christian vocation. These are the remarks which God inspires in the prayer that contemplates Christ. They are what the Holy Spirit can convey to the Church when the Church listens and receives her specific vocation. Consequently, these revelations are among the most difficult to hear, in that they reveal both a mission and a sin. They are an opening on what Christians refer to as "the mystery of Israel."[1]

I return to three points in the second chapter of Saint Matthew, and will deal with three protagonists: the children of Bethlehem, Herod, and, finally, Christ.

I leave aside the Wise Men, because they are precisely those who will benefit most from all that is set in motion; that which I would like to share with you is thus a reflection situated within the point of view of the Christian faith.

---

1. Among these Christians, Jacques Maritain, who in 1937 wrote a preface to the work of E. Peterson's *Le mystère des Juifs et des Gentils dans l'Église*, collection "Courrier des Iles," nx. 6 (Paris: Desclée de Brouwer, 1935). Léon Bloy and Charles Journet also wrote works on the mystery of Israel.

The Massacre of the Children of Bethlehem:
The Suffering of Israel

We must believe that all the suffering of Israel, persecuted by pagans because of its Election, is a part of the Messiah's suffering, just as the killing of the children in Bethlehem makes up a part of Christ's Passion. Otherwise, God himself would appear incoherent regarding his promise to Israel.

If Christian theology is unable to inscribe in its vision of the Redemption, of the mystery of the Cross, that Auschwitz also makes up a part of Christ's suffering, then we have reached the summit of absurdity. The persecution of God's Chosen is not a crime like other crimes of which mankind is capable. It is a crime directly linked to the Election and, therefore, to the Jewish condition. We must be willing to go that far in our understanding of these events.

It is precisely because of this initial "setting aside" of Israel that the nations have persecuted it, regardless of the practical and historical conditions that have resulted from this persecution and regardless of the practical, social, and cultural consequences that might have provoked or explained such attitudes.

The words I have just spoken can only be said, can only be thought, by Christ's disciples, in their prayer before the crucified Christ. These words can have meaning only for those followers of the crucified Jesus who accept to share his Passion. These words are a part of Christ's secret which is entrusted solely to his disciples. And when this secret is revealed to the world, it provokes derision, insult, the spittle of disgust. It is ridiculed. This secret — for it truly is a secret — can only be borne in compassion with Christ. This secret can be recognized only in faith, because it concerns the very idea we have of God. It means pushing the scandal of the Passion to its limit. It evokes, shockingly and provocatively, the meditation of Psalm 22: "My God, my God, why hast thou forsaken me?" It drives the disciple of Christ up against a wall, where he can only listen to the Father's silence and share this silence with the Son. It compels the disciple to receive Christ's dead body in his arms. Consequently, it plunges us into the scandal of faith, where our faith falters, where our faithfulness itself is tested and its only re-course is Christ's faithfulness, when the only way to endure such a moment is to trust completely in Christ. He alone can bear his Passion in faithfulness. He alone — because he is the Son and he voluntarily enters into this path of obedience — can open for us, by his Passion and his obedience, the meaning of the scandal of Job's suffering and attest that the Father is truly love and faithfulness.

To be able to recognize this is not only a secret but a God-given grace, the very grace of Christian faith and faithfulness. It can be received only in the prayer of those who believe in Christ, the suffering and hidden Messiah.

But even for Israel, its own suffering is an enigma. The Christian cannot explain it to the people of Israel. He can only do as Christ does when he enters into the silence of his Passion. Christ does not explain his Passion: he announces it and enters it in silence. The only way in which he invites his disciples to understand it is to follow him. And the only way the disciples respond is by running away. The measure of their unfaithfulness is Christ's Passion. Not one of his disciples has the strength to follow Christ in his Passion, not even those he has specifically invited to do so. The disciples can follow Christ in his Passion only at the price of forgiveness — the forgiveness given to Peter and the grace given by the Risen Christ who shows his wounds and bestows the Holy Spirit.

For Israel, its own suffering is a scandal that leads it either to stumble in its faith or else to place its trust, still more obscurely and more incomprehensibly, in God's faithfulness. How, at the end of history, will God recognize in his Christ all those who have been given to him? It is the unfathomable mystery of his mercy.

Herod's Point of View: The Pagan's Sin

The massacre and the persecution of Israel by the pagan nations — we must not hesitate to say, by "pagan-Christians" — are the test of their lie or of their feigned worship of Christ.

Herod says to the Wise Men, "Bring me word, that I too may come and worship him" (Matthew 2:8). He pretends that he wants to recognize the Messiah, but, in reality, he has the children of Bethlehem killed. He thus reveals his true identity: a liar. His feigned worship of the Messiah is a lie. The massacre of the children of Bethlehem is the proof of Herod's lie. And, similarly, one can say that the concrete attitude of the pagan-Christian societies and authorities toward the people of Israel is the symptom of their genuine unfaithfulness to Christ; or of their lie in their pseudo-faithfulness to Christ. Their attitude is an unintended avowal of their paganism and their sin.

In this case, we are dealing with a very specific sin, one which touches God himself. It is not simply a matter of the horror which is usual for the human species, which never hesitates to kill, massacre, and behave in ways unworthy of God and of mankind. Throughout history, no one people can be said to be more evil than another — it would be difficult to award a prize!

But the persecution of Israel is not simply a variation — specific to Western countries, or to Israel, or a small corner of humanity — of that evil which is common tender throughout history. The history of the persecution of Israel is distinct in that it is not in the same category as the crimes commonly committed by men and to which all peoples are vulnerable — since even previously pacific groups can transform themselves into executioners. Here we are dealing with the designation of the absolute victim.

If the pagan-Christians have dared to speak of deicide regarding Israel and Christ — when the Gospel clearly states that the responsibility for Christ's death was taken by all, Jewish and Roman authorities, facing the fickleness of the people of Jerusalem — then we ought to speak of deicide in the case of the so-called Christian peoples of the West, and the fate they inflicted on the Jewish people. For, in this case, what applies to one applies to the other: a refusal of Christ as he offers himself, a hate of the Election as God gives it. This is the test of the pagan-Christians' lie in their pretended faithfulness to God. Hence, this is sin.

We have to penetrate yet further into this reasoning. The unmasking of the depth of this sin can be borne only in prayer, and can only be received as a grace in prayer. Otherwise, the truth is either refused — that is, we prefer to ignore it — or else induces a crushing feeling of guilt.

Facing such a crime, these are the two usual solutions: either to close our eyes to it, which is the phenomenon of callousness, or else to be overwhelmed by guilt, which is a suicidal attitude, that of Judas Iscariot. But whether it is a refusal to see or suicide when facing the weight of evil, neither attitude is bearable, neither is Christian, neither is of Christ. When Christ reveals the depth of sin, it is to forgive and redeem it.

The Christian conscience, that of Christ's disciples, must be capable of recognizing, in prayer, this sin committed by our brothers, peoples with whom we share a responsibility across history. Only thus — united with Christ, the suffering and hidden Messiah — can the Christian conscience bear such a crime in prayer. The executioners of the people of Israel can be viewed only from one point: on the Cross with Christ. There is no other perspective from which we can view them. This is what Mary does, as she stands at the foot of the Cross. Otherwise, we react like the apostles: we leave, we run away. If we see the executioners other than as Jesus sees them, we, too, become executioners. This is what the pagan-Christians did when they chose to designate a single executioner, the Jews, whereas the Gospel clearly states that it was the pagans who crucified Christ.[2] The pagan-Christians killed the Jews under the pretext that the Jews killed Christ. This is an outright blasphemy, a clear revelation that they were motivated by the spirit of the world and not the spirit of Christ. It is the power of Satan, who "was a murderer from the beginning" (John 8:44), under which they acted. As a result, they are responsible for the fact that the Messiah is unrecognizable and unknown to both Jews and pagans.

The only position from which such a realization can be borne, when God's grace to do so is given, is to remain with Christ, in the atti-

---

2. Cf. Matthew 27:26, 27-31; Mark 15:15, 16-20; Luke 23:24-25; John 19:16, 23, 32-34.

tude of Mary or the beloved disciple, who enter into the Messiah's secret and share his Passion for the forgiveness of sins.

Twenty centuries of history in the Western world shed a violent light on all this. But the substance of everything I have been saying can be found, almost literally, in the New Testament writings, even though it cannot be said that these writings prophesy the events that followed (such an affirmation would be utterly stupid). The mystery of Christ covers, like a layer of light, all history to come. Certainly, it would be absurd to use the Scripture in a material way, wanting to use specific words to designate specific events. But it is clear that Scripture does foretell this our time, until the end of time, since the mystery of Christ anticipates the totality of history.

When Jesus says to his disciples in the apocalyptic discourse (Matthew 24:9), "And you will be hated by all nations (the *goyim*) for my name's sake," he is accurately describing the disciples' place at the Messiah's side. It remains to understand, in Christ, why and how. According to what logic? But it is surely this very mystery that is also referred to in Jesus' teaching concerning our time as opposed to the time to come, concerning this "time of the nations" when the disciples themselves will experience Christ's Passion, and, in order to bear it, will receive the strength of the Holy Spirit and, already, the first-fruits of the Resurrection.

Christ's Point of View: The Compassion of the Disciple

To cope with this double mystery — the mystery of the killing of the children, the mystery of evil and of Herod's lie — the disciple of Christ is given the grace to be of Christ, and hence to receive his strength, his grace, and his Spirit and, already, his resurrected life, as his hope.

Otherwise, just as, when confronted with the revelation of sin, we could only flee or deny it, so, before the suffering vocation of the Messiah, we can only refuse it or flee once again, like the disciples and contemporaries of Jesus.

It is only through the grace of the gift of the Spirit and the grace of the Messiah and of his Resurrection that hope becomes possible. The way to hope is opened only when we share Jesus' own vocation.

This vocation can be realized in a vocation of prayer, and of prayer within the Church — of prayer for both Israel and the Gentile nations, in Christ's compassion.

When Thomas says, "Unless I see in his hands the print of the nails, . . . I will not believe" and Jesus responds, "Put your finger here, and see my hands; and put out your hand, and place it in my side," Jesus is inviting him, in a certain way, to this attitude of compassion with him.[3]

What the Risen Christ is proposing to Thomas is that he enter into Christ's Passion so as to share in the passion of Israel. What has been endured as an incomprehensible misfortune becomes, through prayer, a redemptive action. It does not mean putting ourselves in the victim's place, but rather becoming a part of Christ. It does not mean feeling pity for the children of Bethlehem — which would be a purely sentimental transfer to rid oneself of guilt — but entering into Christ's Passion if we are called on to do so. And every baptized person is called to do so, according to the measure of grace given to him by God. Compassion does not signify pity or sympathy, but is a God-given grace allowing us to share in his Son's Passion, in our acceptance, in faith, that God bestows the form of the Passion on our lives, even if our lives unfold within a peaceful context.

The Christian vocation, in the most fundamental and rigorous sense of the word, finds here an extremely powerful meaning: sharing in the Passion of Christ who bears his people's suffering and works toward the redemption of the world.

This prayer is a prayer for the pagans, that they may receive Christ's forgiveness, for those pagans who may be called Christians, but who took possession of Christianity to make it into their religion, and disfigured it.

A Jesuit missionary to Latin America expressed this disfigurement in these words: "They took our Christ; they made him their god." The assimilating power of civilizations and of peoples reduces the

---

3. Cf. John 20:24-29.

Christian faith received to the contents of archaic religions. The same thing happened with Israel and the Canaanite forms of worship. Paganism was constantly fought by the prophets, the priests, and the faithful of Israel, in their struggle to bring the people to repentance. Israel's long struggle to distance itself from the pagan religions allowed it to realize over time and to receive the grace of that which God wanted it to discover: the holiness to which it had been called for the salvation of all mankind.

However, paganism always remains a temptation, in its most archaic as well as its most developed forms. The power that man has given himself is the most subtle and most modern of these temptations.

Paganism remains a reality with which the disciples of Christ are constantly being confronted.

Not all baptized pagans have taken the same path as Israel. The water of baptism has not yet penetrated to their hearts. Their true conversion would presume a much more profound progression, a radical change in their mores and life. A church is not created solely by hanging a cross on the wall of a pagan temple, nor is a Christian empire created merely by drawing a cross on a flag.

Prayer for the pagans, prayer that they may be given Christ's forgiveness, is also a prayer for their repentance. For there to be forgiveness, there must be repentance. The first grace of forgiveness is to elicit contrition in man's heart and thus lead him to the discovery of sin. To pray that repentance will come, that the sin will be recognized, that God will forgive; all this is a part of the Church's supplication.

But this is a specifically Christian point of view. I repeat and insist: this point of view is understandable and bearable only when facing the Crucified Christ, or the Risen Christ showing us his wounds. It makes sense only within a Christian and ecclesial act of faith, and cannot take place outside of it. The grace that can flow from this prayer for the Church is to discover her specific and original vocation, in a way that is much fuller, purer, and stronger, and to receive that vocation as a grace from God.

In those cases where the Church has practically identified herself with pagan Christianity, she sees it collapse when faced with its own criticism, which leads to a loss of faith, and seeing this she loses sight of her own Christian identity.

The explanation in part is that, in these cases, the Church has cut herself off from her Jewish roots by transforming Christ into the form of her own paganism, into a pagan deity. But facing the Church is Israel, which bears witness to God — and not to Christ. The Church can receive Christ only if she recognizes Israel, because Christ is the Messiah of Israel. The Church must bear witness to Christ before both pagans and Jews, but she can do this only by sharing the condition of Christ, who is crucified, hidden and mysterious. And to the extent to which the Church tries to reject Israel as the enemy, it is in fact her Christ that she is refusing.

The Church's crucified and crucifying position can be lived only in that hope which announces, in our time and in our world, the fulfillment, already realized but still hidden, of the promises made to Israel, buried until the Son of Man appears in his glory. In order that the grace given to Israel appear as the source of salvation for all, Christ, the Son of God, unites pagans and Jews in his grace. Thus, God's faithfulness is made manifest. He brings together his Son's disciples in order that they may have the grace to share in his destiny and to become, in their turn, the sacrament of this hope.

The sin to which the pagan-Christians, whether representatives of the Church or princes or peoples, have succumbed has been to take possession of Christ in disfiguring him and then to make this distortion into their god. They have thus brought persecuted Israel to appear, in spite of itself, as a figure of the humiliated Christ. Their failure to recognize Israel is the test of their failure to recognize the Christ they claim to serve.

CHAPTER 6

In Him, All God's Promises Are Fulfilled

In chapter 3 of Saint Matthew, John the Baptist comes to preach in the wilderness of Judea: "Repent, for the kingdom of heaven is at hand." He is the one of whom Isaiah the prophet spoke: "The voice of one crying in the wilderness: 'Prepare the way of the Lord; make his paths straight.'" Saint Matthew describes John the Baptist as dressed like Elijah, in camel's hair, with a leather girdle around his waist, nourishing himself on locusts and honey. Are these mere details? Not at all. We shall return to this point. But let us continue with the narrative: "Then went out to him Jerusalem and all Judea and all the region about the Jordan, and they were baptized by him in the river Jordan, confessing their sins. But when he saw many of the Pharisees and Sadducees coming for baptism, he said to them, 'You brood of vipers! Who warned you to flee from the wrath to come? Bear fruit that befits repentance, and do not presume to say to yourselves, 'We have Abraham as our father'; for I tell you, God is able from these stones to raise up children to Abraham. Even now the axe is laid to the root of the trees; every tree therefore that does not bear good fruit is cut down and thrown into the fire. I baptize you with water for repentance, but he who is coming after me is mightier than I, whose sandals I am not worthy to carry; he will baptize you with the Holy Spirit and with fire. His winnowing fork is in his hand, and he will clear his threshing floor and gather his wheat into the granary, but the chaff he will burn with unquenchable fire.'" Then Jesus appears, coming from Galilee to the banks of the Jordan, to be baptized by John. But John tries to dissuade him, saying, "I need to be baptized by you, and do you come to me?" Jesus answers, "Let it be so now; for thus it is fitting for us to fulfill all righteousness." Then John consents. "And when Jesus was baptized, he went up immediately from the water, and behold, the heavens were opened and he saw the Spirit of God descending like a dove, and alighting on him; and lo, a voice from heaven, saying, 'This is my beloved Son, with whom I am well pleased.' Then Jesus was led up by the Spirit into the wilderness to be tempted by the devil. And he fasted forty days and forty nights, and afterward he was hungry" (Matthew 3:5-17; 4:1-27).

There follows the account of the three temptations. "Then the devil left him, and behold, angels came and ministered to him" (Matthew 4:11).

"Now when he heard that John had been arrested, he withdrew into Galilee; and leaving Nazareth he went and dwelt in Capernaum by the sea, in the territory of Zebulun and Naphtali, that what was spoken by the prophet Isaiah might be fulfilled: 'The land of Zebulun and the land of Naphtali, toward the sea, across the Jordan, Galilee of the Gentiles — the people who sat in darkness have seen a great light, and for those who sat in the region of the shadow of death light has dawned'" (Matthew 4:12-16).

Jesus' ministry begins only after his temptation in the wilderness and John's arrest.

"From that time Jesus began to preach, saying, 'Repent, for the kingdom of heaven is at hand'" (Matthew 4:17). The baptism of Jesus and his temptation in the wilderness thus belong to the hidden mysteries. And these moments of the Gospel must be received in an attitude of contemplation and prayer; otherwise, we cannot grasp what is being said.

The Baptism of John

Let us take a closer look at several points.

First of all, what is the nature of John the Baptist's baptism? What is its significance and importance for the Church? This baptism is a capital event in the Gospel, which has retained all its power; but it is often misunderstood or ignored, because it is regarded as only a vague preparation, a kind of penitential rite to "set things in order," similar to what one might do before Christmas or Easter!

In fact, the baptism given by John is indeed the origin of the baptism with which we are all baptized. It is the baptism received by Jesus and subsequently by us, too. It is the same fundamental act that inaugurates the kingdom of heaven. Because John the Baptist — Saint Matthew says it expressly (3:2) — announces that the kingdom of heaven is at hand; Jesus repeats the same announcement almost literally (Matthew 4:17). This point is also emphasized by John the Evangelist.

What is the meaning of John the Baptist's teaching and the baptism he offers?

John the Baptist is presented as the new Elijah by Saint Matthew: "Now John wore a garment of camel's hair, and a leather girdle around his waist; and his food was locusts and wild honey" (Matthew 3:4).

His dress and nourishment are clear allusions to Elijah, the prophet: "'What kind of man was he who came to meet you and told you these things?' They answered him, 'He wore a garment of haircloth, with a girdle of leather about his loins.' And he said, 'It is Elijah the Tishbite'" (2 Kings 1:7-8).

Jesus himself designates John the Baptist in this way when speaking to the crowds: "And if you are willing to accept it, he is Elijah who is to come" (Matthew 11:14 and 17:12: "... has already come"). According to Jewish belief, the return of Elijah precedes the coming of the Messiah.

Is there a precedent in Judaism to the baptism given by John the Baptist? It is neither the ablutions of Qumran nor the ordinary Jewish ritual ablutions. The only reference which would have meaning here is the baptism of proselytes. In the contemporary Judaism that was in full expansion across the Roman Empire, there were many "God-fearing," that is, pagans who wanted to enter the Covenant. Was circumcision, for which they felt a strong repugnance, to be required of them? In the first or near the end of the second century B.C., the practice spread of using baptism as a substitute for circumcision when incorporating pagans into Israel — in the hope that later these converts would have their own children circumcised. Unfortunately, in practice, this led to many abuses and subsequently Judaism curbed the practice. To thwart it, a celebrated rabbi of the time gave this advice: "Very well, we baptize them, but we circumcise them first," because pagans tended to see the rite of baptism as an easier path, and would subsequently shirk their religious obligations.

But the baptismal rite is not just any rite; it has a meaning; it is the rite which pagans undergo to become incorporated into Israel.

Yet John the Baptist initially proposes this rite exclusively to the inhabitants of Jerusalem, Judea, and the territories bordering the Jordan, and not to the inhabitants of Samaria, or even those of Galilee. The evangelists stress the fact that John the Baptist will go only later to Samaria, to prepare it, through his preaching, for the eschatological reunion of the two kingdoms of Judea and Samaria: he will precede Christ there, having prepared those who will become his disciples. Jesus says this explicitly: "I sent you to reap that for which you did not labor; others have labored, and you have entered into their labor" (John 4:35-38). In Jesus' words, the one who sowed is John the Baptist.

For the moment, however, John the Baptist is proposing to the Judeans a baptism of repentance in view of conversion: they must consider themselves like pagans since they have broken the Covenant and can now enter it again by the pure grace of God.

By confessing their sin, they ask God to reestablish the Covenant, to grant the New Covenant announced by Jeremiah and Ezekiel. In this Covenant the Holy Spirit will inscribe the Law in the hearts of the people, and make it so that Israel will sin no more: Israel will be an entirely holy people, because God's own power will dwell in it in fullness, according to the prayer expressed in Deuteronomy. One can say that the whole Gospel is already contained in Deuteronomy, as a hope that God will fulfill. It is in Deuteronomy that we find all the texts that form the heart of Jewish piety and thus of Jesus' faith, including "Hear O Israel."[1] It is in Deuteronomy that Jesus finds his answers to the tempter. This is not by chance.

We can say that all God's Promise, the proclamation of the Good News, is already there: God will come, will bestow his Spirit, and will make it possible for Israel to obey God, to perform this service in love and thus accomplish the work of holiness by which the world will be saved. Because if Israel thus obeys God, having received from him the strength to do so, then the Promise will be fulfilled. God will change men's hearts by coming himself to dwell in Israel's heart and by making Israel his obedient and loving son.

It is up to Israel, to the inhabitants of Judea, to recognize themselves as having no "rights" before God, as sinners. They, who have received the Covenant, have to give these privileges up to God and rely completely on God's power so that he can save them freely, as if they were pagans, although they are Jews. This is perhaps the paradoxical sense of John's baptism for the remission of sins.

John the Baptist sees coming toward him many Pharisees and Sadducees, that is, people who hold completely contradictory opinions: some believe in the resurrection, others do not; their positions are irreconcilable. And this is indeed the sense of John's preaching: "You brood of vipers! Who warned you to flee from the wrath to come?" The judgment of God. "Bear fruit that befits repentance, and do not presume to say to yourselves, 'We have Abraham as our father'; for I tell you, God is able from these stones to raise up children to Abraham" (Matthew 3:7-9). This could be an allusion to the resurrection, because the "stones" could also refer to erected stones, tombstones. It is the unmerited aspect of God's gift that is being pointed out: the recognition that being sons of Abraham gives no rights and that God can resurrect the children of Abraham. "God is able from these stones to

---

1. The book of Deuteronomy is highly prized by Judaism. The library in Qumran had more than fifteen copies. It contains the most perfected synthesis of Old Testament theology, presented, according to von Rad, "in an incomparable equilibrium which will never again be achieved." It is the book most cited in the New Testament, after the Psalms and Isaiah.

raise up children to Abraham" means that God is going to raise the dead. Therefore, you must be ready for conversion and to receive the time of judgment. "The axe is laid to the root of the trees, every tree therefore that does not bear good fruit is cut down and thrown into the fire" (Matthew 3:10).

John announces this kingdom which is at hand: "I baptize you with water for repentance, but he who is coming after me is mightier than I, whose sandals I am not worthy to carry" (Matthew 3:11). Since carrying sandals is the gesture of the disciple who serves his master, he says: I am not even worthy to be his disciple. "He follows me." He comes after me. "He is mightier than I." "And he will baptize you with the Holy Spirit and with fire" — the fire of the Spirit, the purifying fire which allows one to stand before the judgment. It is the announcement of a total and definitive purification from sin. It is the announcement of the fullness of the gift of the Holy Spirit and of the holiness that God wants to grant his people.

This verse is followed by the announcement of the eschatological judgment of which the harvest is a metaphor, whereas the sowing represents our time of history.

Then Jesus appears, coming from Galilee. He who until then has been "put in reserve" comes to the banks of the Jordan to be baptized by John. At first, John protests: "I need to be baptized by you" (Matthew 3:14). In saying this, John recognizes, identifies, and designates Jesus as the one who baptizes in the Spirit and in fire.

Jesus' response is capital: "Let it be so for the moment" — for this time, the time of his life — "for thus it is fitting for us to fulfill all righteousness" (Matthew 3:15). The "us" demonstrates the absolute solidarity between the fates of John the Baptist and Jesus. John will anticipate the Passion of Jesus.

Then come the two scenes to which the preamble has led us: Jesus' baptism and his triple temptation.

Jesus Is Baptized

In a true revelation, an apocalypse, we hear the voice of God who speaks — words destined only for Jesus, at least for the moment, as he himself will remind the crowds in chapter 11, verse 27: "All things have been delivered to me by my Father; and no one knows the Son except the Father, and no one knows the Father except the Son and any one to whom the Son chooses to reveal him."

This revelation of Jesus as Son who receives the fullness of God's Spirit and is designated by God as the true Son, in whom God takes delight, can be understood on two different levels which, far from excluding each other, are mutually complementary, for neither can be realized without the other.

The most obvious level of meaning is that Jesus is designated as the Son *par excellence*. He is designated not as a substitute for Israel, but as the very realization of Israel's vocation. He is the one in whom the Promise destined for all of Israel is realized and by whom it can be communicated.

Moreover, this is what the following parts of the narrative will continue to symbolize. In fact, the temptations of Jesus in the wilderness, the symbolism of the numbers and the temptations, will echo the Exodus, the wandering of the people of Israel in the wilderness. This parallel is neither accidental nor simply the result of a taste for harmony. It is meant to indicate in a very precise way that in Jesus the promise has been realized because he is the beloved and obedient Son, capable of fully accomplishing the Father's will in the combat of faithfulness. And this is so because he has received the plenitude of the Spirit and God has realized in him the prophetic promise.

This means that in Jesus all of God's promises will be realized, up to and including death defeated, since that is a part of Israel's hope: holiness, the vision of God face to face, the resurrection of the dead, the gathering together of the people in its land and the fulfillment of all the eschatological promises.

Jesus is designated by the evangelist as the one in whom is fully accomplished, albeit in the secret of our present existence, the totality of the hope of Israel.

The second level of meaning is that this beloved Son, the name given to him in the Heavenly Father's love, will be revealed to us as the very Word of God, the eternal Son of God made flesh. He is Son in an unimaginable sense. In him, Israel not only comes face to face with God, but Jesus is the very one in whom God's Glory dwells, the one in whom this Glory not only becomes the spoken, heard word, but becomes Word made flesh. God in his Son offers himself up for us, and offers up his Son to us. Obviously, this can be believed only by those to whom this grace is given by Christ himself. This belief is not a merit about which one could boast. Jesus tells us: "All things have been delivered to me by my Father; and no one knows the Son except the Father, and no one knows the Father except the Son and anyone to whom the Son chooses to reveal him" (Matthew 11:27).

Similarly, the Son's secret is known only to the Father and to those to whom the Father wishes to reveal it. This is what will be said explicitly to Peter once he has recognized Jesus as the Messiah, the Son of the living God — regardless of what Peter's words may have meant to him at the time. Jesus says to him, "Blessed are you, Simon Bar-Jona! For flesh and blood has not revealed this to you, but my Father who is in heaven" (Matthew 16:17). Jesus recognizes in Peter's confession of faith the word of grace that had been addressed to him.

The recognition of the Son in his filial condition can only be the work of God. Thus it can be received only as a gift of grace, granted by the Father and, hence, as a vocation. It cannot be the object of a demonstration; the only demonstration of the Son's condition is the Cross. Saint John himself will say that there, on the Cross, are revealed the Glory of God and the filiation of Jesus.[2]

Thus is presented the one who truly submits himself to John's baptism. He receives the Covenant. He inaugurates the time of the Covenant in the Spirit of God, which he will accomplish by an act of pure receptivity, pure submission. Not by feigning to consider himself a sin-

2. Cf. John 12:23-28.

65

ner, but by recognizing that the gift given to Israel itself is freely bestowed by God, that even he, the Son of God, has no "right" to it; that everything is given as pure grace of the Father. He submits himself to baptism, this rite of the Covenant, which connotes submersion and death, as well as reemergence and life. Another parallel in which, from the beginning, his vocation as the suffering Messiah appears, or we might say, his "condition as the suffering servant," since there is no direct reference to the Messiah here, except perhaps with the use of the term "son," which can also be a term of royalty (cf. Psalm 2).[3]

Being the Son, he receives the Father's love as pure grace. And it is in full and total obedience that he accomplishes his time in the wilderness.

The Triple Temptation

The first temptation faced by Jesus, as related by the evangelist, consists in accepting to receive his life from God alone rather than from his own strength; to recognize that God is indeed the source of life and the only source of life, that the Word of God is therefore able to conquer death and that this Word must be received and kept as faithfully as possible, to the very limits of life. Because when Jesus is hungry, that does not simply mean he is feeling hunger, appetite, but that his very life is threatened. He accepts to remain under this threat so as to put his faith exclusively in God's Word, which is his nourishment, his life.

The same is true for the fulfillment of God's will. "If you are the Son of God, throw yourself down; for it is written, 'He will give his angels charge of you,' and 'On their hands they will bear you up, lest you strike your foot against a stone' (Psalm 91)" (Matthew 4:6). Here again,

3. In his account of the Suffering Servant, Isaiah evokes the figure as "a lamb that is led to slaughter" and "taken away," "cut off from the land of the living," but because of his suffering, this servant "shall see his offspring" and "prolong his days"; cf. Isaiah 53:7-11. John the Baptist designates Jesus both as "Lamb of God" and "the Chosen"; cf. John 1:29, 34-36.

in the very fulfillment of God's will, the obedient Son refuses to appropriate God's plan. He submits himself completely, refusing to turn this plan into anything else than that which was destined by God. The Son remains in the filial condition of loving obedience and, thus, of faith. The Letter to the Hebrews refers to Christ as the "pioneer and perfecter of our faith" (Hebrews 12:2). Here we find an important aspect of Christian theology, which is often overlooked. The "endurance" of Christ (Hebrews 12:2, 3) is the fulfillment of the attitude to which Israel is called and which Christ's disciples live in "faith."

Jesus' response is: "You shall not tempt the Lord your God" (Matthew 4:7).

The third temptation is a reenactment and summary of Israel's conflict with every human social figure: how can Israel receive its condition, collectively and as a people, its temporal and physical existence, from any other than God alone? The devil leaves Jesus until the time when the ordeal will be renewed: "And behold, angels came and ministered to him" (Matthew 4:11).

The Good News

Jesus withdraws to Galilee, the evangelist tells us, and he emphasizes — by quoting the prophecies of Isaiah — that we are dealing with the "Galilee of the Gentiles," the Galilee of the pagans. The obedient servant thus becomes, as the prophet had said, the light of the pagan nations. He brings light, that is, life to the Gentiles, who are subject to death. He brings life, which is not only the Law but also resurrection.

It is because Jesus lives the obedience which God expects of Israel that he can thus accomplish that for which God has destined Israel. This is mentioned many times in the Bible. Luke says it, in his manner, through Simeon's prophecy: "A light for revelation to the Gentiles, and for glory to thy people Israel" (Luke 2:32). "The people who sat in darkness have seen a great light, and for those who sat in the region and the shadow of death light has dawned" (Matthew 4:16). This quotation is taken almost word for word from Isaiah (9:1) and is repeated in part by Luke (1:79) at the end of Zechariah's prophecy. Obviously, it was referring to the cult of idols, but also to death in the strict sense of the word.

Rather than being a preamble to the Gospel, the story of Jesus' presentation at the Temple, as described by Saint Luke, can be considered as a kind of "vestibule," before Jesus begins to preach. In this vestibule, Jesus is revealed as the one in whom God fulfills the promise made to Israel. The point emphasized here is the gift of the Spirit and the victory over Satan, the adversary. It is the gift of the Spirit and faithfulness, or faith, brought to its perfection: we can speak of Jesus' faith, the accomplishment of Israel's faith; it is the faithfulness of the Son.[4] Symbolically, also, it is the birth of the new people, of the renewed people who, born of the Spirit, is given as a "brother" to this Son, the "first-born among many brethren," as he is referred to by Saint Paul in the Letter to the Romans.[5]

In the light of what we have seen in "Jesus and the Law," let us return to this point.

Christ's delight is in the divine Law; he has nourished himself by its total fulfillment, he who has told us that nothing must be omitted from it, not even the least of the commandments. The "Good News" is that the promised Spirit, which grants faithfulness to Israel, rests in fullness upon Jesus. The gift is the object of both our hope and of our faith. In Jesus, the faithfulness promised by God to Israel has already been realized — Jesus observes the Law in its totality and to perfection. Not in the way that men can observe it, but as the Son filled with the Spirit of God, who observes it in the sovereign liberty of God, making it a personal, inner law, his nourishment. In the sovereign freedom of the Spirit, he accomplishes the totality of the Law in perfection, finding in it the mystery of God's love and the face of the Father.

---

4. Christ's faith is to be understood according to the thought of Hans Urs von Balthasar in *La Foi du Christ. Cinq Approches Christologiques* (Paris: Aubier Montaigne, 1968). See also John Greehey and Matthew Vellanickal, who evoke the "filial faith" of Jesus in "Le caractère unique et singulier de Jésus comme Fils de Dieu" (Commission biblique pontificale, *Bible et christologie* [Paris: Cerf, 1984], pp. 173-196).

5. Cf. Romans 8:29; see also Hebrews 2:10.

It is therefore Jesus who simultaneously fulfills the promise of the forgiveness of sin and the transformation of the human heart. He is that human being with a "new heart," on whom sin has no hold, who therefore can fulfill the Law perfectly and who lives it completely.[6] He is the one for whom the Law will no longer be a revelation of sin, but rather a revelation of grace. Because to a sinful and weak man, incapable of accomplishing God's will, the Law reveals the extent of his unfaithfulness, and his only recourse is to implore God's mercy. Whereas in Christ, the Law reveals love, since he fully accomplishes it and, in the gift of the Spirit, he communes fully with the Father's will. Within him dwells the fullness of the Spirit, as was promised to Israel. There is no sin in him, and he is not subject to judgment. He is even the one by whom that judgment takes place, since he is holiness itself: he alone can measure sin and face sin. But how?

This, the Gospel teaches us, is the mystery of the one who "was made to be sin for us."[7] How can God and man pit themselves against sin? It is something we cannot imagine. To quote Isaiah's words: "We esteemed him stricken, smitten by God, and afflicted. But he was wounded for our transgression; he was bruised for our iniquities" (Isaiah 53:4-5).

Since he has been given to us, since the Kingdom of God is at hand, the invitation is thus extended to us, open to all those whom God calls to believe in this Good News and to receive the first-fruits and the pledge of what is already fully accomplished in him.

That which is given in Jesus is already communicated to us, albeit in the form of hope, in the form of a deposit.[8] We believe that this gift is already given by God, that it is buried in the secret of this time, and that, already, we can participate in it through God's grace. Even if we remain sinners and are constantly reclaimed by what Saint Paul calls the "old nature," by the forces of death that dwell in us and which the Spirit has not yet fully overcome in us,[9] we live in the time when the

---

6. Cf. Ezekiel 36:26: "A new heart I will give you."
7. The expression is Saint Paul's: cf. 2 Corinthians 5:21.
8. Cf. 2 Corinthians 1:22; 5:5.
9. Cf. Ephesians 4:22; Colossians 3:9.

harvest is yet to come. That which is so far given only as a seed and a sprout, according to the diversity of hearts and their secret, has yet to ripen for the harvest that God will gather into his storehouse.

To believe this is the specifity of the Christian faith, the faith of Christ's disciples. It is unfortunate and rather strange that the word *Christian* should have become, in current language, a word taken as directly antagonistic to the word *Jew*. These two words are not on the same plane. A "Christian" is a disciple of Christ, or, let us say, a disciple of Jesus (which leaves aside the question of Israel and the pagans). One can become a Christian only by acknowledging this condition as a grace. Just as the inhabitants of Judea, the Jews of Judea and Jerusalem, the Pharisees and the Sadducees of Jesus' time were invited to welcome this promised fulfillment of God's reign as a freely bestowed grace of which they were unworthy. John the Baptist's message was not new; it was already completely given in the prophets: "Change our hearts, Lord, and we shall be changed"; "Restore us to thyself, O LORD, that we may be restored!" (Lamentations 5:21). So many phrases of Hosea, Jeremiah, Isaiah, and Baruch say it abundantly.[10] Such words are the very foundation of the prophetic predication from the moment where the experience of infidelity was made, and at the same time the experience of trust in God's power.

The disciples of Jesus know that they presently share, still only as a hope yet nonetheless in reality, the gift made in Jesus. They can become brothers, disciples, members of his body, and thus participate in what is in him the perfection of God's gift. They know that the Kingdom of God has arrived, not in its eschatological fulfillment, but by the gift of the Spirit, in the one who is risen from the dead and who, already, shares his life with us.

10. For example, Hosea 14:2; Isaiah 44:21-23; Jeremiah 31:18; Baruch 2:31, 32; 4:28, 29.

CHAPTER 7

The Hope of Israel

B efore going on, I should like to return to some of the multiple consequences and treasures which chapter 3 of Saint Matthew's Gospel can evoke in us.

Jesus is presented by the evangelist, who is addressing the disciples' faith, as the one in whom the promise made to Israel is accomplished. Not as a substitute for Israel, but as the fulfillment of Israel. He
is both Israel's hope, given as an anticipation of the final coming and of
the end of time, and the one in whom Israel will be able to recognize its
own destiny. He is also the one in whom the Gentiles will be able to
hope, because he is the "Light of the Gentile nations."

It is clear, in this respect, that the Spirit of Jesus can be received
only on the strict condition of sharing the hope of Israel and having access to it. This is the meaning of baptism, since in baptism — according to Saint Paul's expression — we are "incorporated" into Christ.[1]
But baptism is at the same time, and inseparably — otherwise it would
be meaningless — an incorporation into Israel.

The fact that today many Jews do not recognize this is quite another question. The question with which we are dealing here is to
know how the disciple of Christ can receive this and believe it, the con-

1. Cf. 1 Corinthians 12:13-27; Ephesians 1:23; 3:6; 4:12; Colossians 1:18, 24.

ditions under which a disciple truly believes it. It is up to us to assume and receive the faith according to the wealth which God gives to us, and the specific grace thus bestowed on us.

Clearly, it is impossible to share Israel's hope without having shared in its purifications. This supposes that the path by which the heart is gradually converted and prepared — up to and including the experience of powerlessness and failure before God's demands — be truly followed. Otherwise, the danger of illusion is immense. Experience and history show that this is no imaginary danger. The danger, if we do not pass by this path of purification, is to receive Christ merely as a new form of the gods that dwell in men's hearts, to turn Christ into the image of our own desire, or to give the gods of the pagans, the gods of the nations, a name which would be that of Christ or of the God of Israel.

Thus, rather than being converted, truly turning back to God, man appropriates God and his revelation and, thus, refuses salvation.

To believe in Christ is precisely to receive, as a grace, the entry into Israel's history, and to receive the fruits of that entry as a free gift of God. Paul underlines this when he writes, "And all were baptized.... For they drank from the supernatural Rock which followed them, and the Rock was Christ" (1 Corinthians 10:2-4), all the while affirming that all that belongs specifically to Israel has not been taken away from it, but is henceforth offered to the pagans as well.[2] There is no shortcut; we cannot do without this path. Otherwise, idolatry will continue to reign.

It results that the Old Testament has not been "invalidated," according to a current expression, by the coming of the Messiah, but, on the contrary, has been made accessible and open to pagans who, without him, would not have had access to it. They share in its hope and riches by Christ who fulfills it. Christ, at the same time, gives them the first-fruits of this hope.

The Old Testament is not a propaedeutic teaching, a literary preface, nor a collection of themes and symbols: it is a true pathway, both

2. Cf. Romans 11:29 and Ephesians 2:19; 3:6.

necessary and relevant — relevant, not because of its anecdotal connections, but by communion and obedience to God, the present spiritual reality of entry into the mystery of the Election.

If the pagans who through Christ have access to the Covenant do not follow Israel's path as revealed in the Old Testament, they risk not being truly converted and, thus, actually despising Christ while believing that they honor him. Herein lies the permanent temptation of the "pagan-Christian peoples." One of the forms of the modern crisis of Christianity is the rejection of its historical root, the rejection of the grace to which Christianity gives access.[3] Following this, the figure of Christ is reduced to a mythical or purely pagan figure of divinity over which Western reason proclaims its triumph.

The way Christ is treated in his historical existence is comparable to the way in which the Word made written word, Scripture, is treated. One of the possible sources of the present crisis of faith in the West is that the God being challenged is nothing other than the god of the pagans disguised as the God of the Christians.

Could it be that Christians in the Western world are now paying the price for a too shallow and rapid conversion? They must be converted more profoundly by the grace they have received in Christ of access to Israel's hope. It is not a matter of going backward, but rather of discovering in Christ all God's riches, to which grace grants us access.

The anti-idolatry polemic of the Old Testament prophets could be compared, perhaps somewhat naively, to the present crisis of secularization and the "Death of God" movement. This means that many Christians have, in their understanding, reduced the God of the Covenant to a mere idol, an idea forged by man himself.

The price to pay for recognizing that God alone is God, and that he is the One God, is the price of a long exodus, of renouncement. Even the simplest, purest, most ignorant soul in Christendom knows very well the cost of praying to God, what renouncement and, often, what dispossession of self, what struggle against illusions, against fear or false images, what a conversion of our hearts is required for access to

---

3. The word *root* is Paulinian: cf. Romans 11:16-18.

the living God. On the other hand, if we imagine that we have grasped God, then, in fact, we have nothing more than an idol between our hands. And then it becomes easy to reduce that idol to an idea and declare it dead. And it is true that it is dead, because it was never alive!

The Gift of the Exodus

Now, let us look again at a long passage from Saint Matthew, beginning with the miracle of the loaves and the fishes (chapter 14) and continuing through the Transfiguration (chapter 17, verse 21). In it Jesus is presented as the fulfillment of Israel's hope, the one in whom this hope has been fulfilled.

After having proposed the perfection of holiness — the fulfillment of God's Law by the gift of the new heart which makes it possible for man to enter thankfully into the Covenant given by God — Jesus organizes the new exodus announced by the prophets.

The symbolism of the numbers and the context of the two miracles of "the loaves and fishes" reported in the Gospels indicate very clearly that one miracle was worked for Israel and the other for the Gentiles, the pagans.

The first multiplication of the loaves is not only the reiteration of Israel's ordeal in the wilderness, but also its full accomplishment, in which the people, called to commune in the New Covenant through the Holy Spirit, receives its life from the Word of God. The condition for access to this New Covenant is the new heart. This can be seen in the discussion that follows with the disciples. Jesus is explicit: "For out of the heart comes purity." It is in man's heart that purity, or its opposite, sin, is found. And it is God who grafts this new plant that will not be uprooted.

Jesus then withdraws into the pagan district of Tyre and Sidon, before returning to the Sea of Galilee, still in pagan territory, on the Decapolis side of the lake. Once again a great crowd converges on him, of the lame, the blind, the deaf and mute: they fall at his feet and he heals them. The crowd is in a state of awe, and on seeing the deaf and mute hear and speak, the lame walk, the blind see, the crowd "glorifies the God of Israel."[4]

The pagans, before the one who has thus accomplished God's Promise, receive healing and salvation; and in glorifying the God of Israel, they, too, are granted access to the Covenant. This is why Jesus will repeat for the pagan crowds the miracle done for Israel in the wilderness: he will nourish them with God's Word. That is the question asked of the Church, already present in the disciples: where can sufficient food be found for all the assembled people? The answer is suggested by Christ himself. If the multitude's hunger is to be satisfied, the food must come from the unique source, from the same source that nourishes Israel. Only the Word of God can satisfy this people by enabling them to escape the trial of death and enter into the hope of life. The food that God gives in the wilderness is the anticipatory sign of the life he will give in heaven.

Here is, already, the guarantee of the hope promised to both Israel and the Gentiles. Israel's hope is doubled by seeing that the Gentiles, symbolized by these people from the pagan Decapolis (a group of ten towns) are called to the Word, whereas Jesus has previously said that he had been "sent only to the lost sheep of the house of Israel."[5] These lost sheep, that is, the scattered sheep of Israel that he brings together, already have the joy of seeing pagans commune in their own riches and receive the same plenitude and the same hope.

The narrative continues with the discussions, first between Jesus and the Pharisees and Sadducees, then with the disciples. The first miracle of the loaves and fishes was followed by a similar explanation. There, Jesus insists that it is faith that will allow the disciples to enter into God's plan, and into the part they are called to take in that plan. Faith in the power of God who gives life, who nourishes, and who unites. He reminds them of the double multiplication of the loaves, of this double sign — for Israel and for the pagans — by showing them the superabundance to which faith can lead.

4. Cf. Matthew 15:29-31.
5. Cf. Matthew 15:24.

Confession of Faith

Next we have the twofold episode of Peter's profession of faith at Caesarea Philippi, and the Transfiguration, which follows the announcement of the Passion.

In order to understand the meaning of the two episodes centered on the figure of Christ, to whom the faith of the Church is addressed, we must not lose sight of the double miracle of the loaves and fishes with the preceding itinerary.

Jesus withdraws with his disciples. "Who do men say that the Son of man is?" (Matthew 16:13). Jesus speaks of himself only in terms which are unique to him, and will not be used by others. He refers to himself as the "Son of Man" of whom the prophet Daniel speaks (Daniel 7:13; 8:15-27; 10:16). Without this reference to Daniel, all these events are incomprehensible. The title "Son of Man" is given to Jesus for his eschatological mission: we shall see the "Son of Man" when he comes on the clouds of heaven, when he comes in his glory. In this sense, the "Son of Man" remains the object of Israel's hope as well as that of the Church.

Jesus himself reinforces Israel's hope by an anticipated fulfillment. Henceforth, both Israel and the people of the New Covenant share the hope that one day "the glory of God" will be revealed, when is seen "a white cloud, and seated on the cloud one like a son of man" (Revelation 14:14), who will inaugurate the ultimate banquet.

Jesus presents himself in the condition of the servant from the first of Isaiah's poems on "the servant" quoted by Saint Matthew: "Behold, my servant whom I uphold. . . . He will not cry or lift up his voice. . . . He will faithfully bring forth justice . . ." (Isaiah 42; Matthew 12:18). Jesus, humble servant, hidden and unrecognized, claims this title, but at the same time he speaks of himself in the third person when designating himself as the "Son of Man." He receives from the Father not this title of "Son of Man," but that of Son of God. The Father calls him "my Son."

"Who do men say that the Son of Man is?" And Simon Peter replies, "You are the Christ, the Son of the living God" (Matthew 16:16). In

designating him as "Christ," the "Lord's Anointed," Peter is again allud-
ing to Daniel (9:26).

He adds a precision in his profession of faith: ". . . the Son of the
living God." Jesus gives thanks for this title which, through Peter's
voice, is bestowed on him by the Father. For Jesus, as Son, never refers
to himself as such. It is always the Father who designates him as his
Son: at his baptism; in Peter's words; at the Transfiguration; and even
in the words of the chief priest: "Tell us if you are Christ, the Son of
God." Jesus replies, "You have said so."[6] For Jesus can receive this title
only from the Father; he cannot call himself thus; he receives himself
as Son only from the Father, even to his most glorious title.

And Jesus says, "Blessed are you Simon Bar-Jonas! For flesh and
blood have not revealed this to you, but my father who is in heaven."

Simon is henceforth a living stone of the new spiritual temple,
the foundation stone of this Assembly, this Church, which is the people of the Covenant that God brings together for the Messiah. People of
the Covenant destined to open to the pagans the riches of Israel, until
Christ comes in glory. "You are Peter, and on this rock" — on this people — "I will build my Church." The word *Church* is not a new word. In
Hebrew it designates the Assembly of Israel in the wilderness. "The
powers of death shall not prevail against it," because the people of the
Most High, of whom the Book of Daniel (12:7-8) speaks, shares in the
destiny of the "Son of Man" and is united to him. Like Jesus himself,
like the Son of Man himself, like the Messiah himself, the holy ones of
the Most High have gone through death and receive the promises of
life. They share in the resurrection: "The powers of death shall not prevail against it." This does not mean that the Church will escape all human vicissitudes. We see how a human understanding of the Church
can lead to a blasphemous interpretation which would consider it an
empire comparable to human empires, one whose power would surpass all others. This way of thinking, shared more or less by all of us, is
typical of a pagan reduction of God's Promise.

Christ says that the Assembly of saints, composed of the sons of

6. Cf. Matthew 26:63, 64.

the saints of which Daniel speaks, having gone through the ordeal of death, will enter into the resurrection: "When the shattering of the power of the holy people comes to an end all these things would be accomplished" (Daniel 12:7). On the other hand, it is not said that the Church will be prosperous, or that in the world's eyes it will be advantageous to be a Christian. In fact, saying that the powers of death will not prevail against the Church means, above all, that the disciples of Jesus will be confronted with death and martyrdom, that they are destined, as Jesus says, to endure the same Passion as he. But even though Jesus' disciples are not destined to triumph on a human level, they will receive from the Father the life force that allows them to confront death in sharing Jesus' Passion. This is the exact opposite of human triumph. It is in the ordeal of suffering, at the height of the Passion on which Israel stumbles, that a divine strength is given to Christ's disciples; it is there that the promise of life, the Resurrection, is already fulfilled as a hope.

The continuation of Jesus' response to Peter — "I will give you the keys of the kingdom of heaven, and whatever you bind on earth shall be bound in heaven, and whatever you loose on earth shall be loosed in heaven" — is the opening, the entrance to the life of God offered to that Assembly who shares Christ's fate. The reference to Daniel (9 to 12) is very important here. It concerns the people of the saints of the Most High, who have passed through death and resurrection and are indissolubly linked to the figure of the "Son of Man," showing how closely Jesus and his Church are tied.

Jesus "strictly charges" his disciples to tell no one that he is the Christ, because this title can be understood only after his Passion is accomplished.

"From that time Jesus began to show his disciples that he must go to Jerusalem and suffer many things from the elders and chief priests and scribes, and be killed, and on the third day be raised. And Peter took him and began to rebuke him, saying, 'God forbid, Lord! This shall never happen to you.' But he turned and said to Peter, 'Get behind me, Satan! You are a hindrance to me; for you are not on the side of God, but of men'" (Matthew 16:21-23).

And he continued to speak to his disciples: "If any man would come after me, let him deny himself and take up his cross and follow me. For whoever would save his life will lose it, and whoever loses his life for my sake will find it. For what will it profit a man, if he gains the whole world and forfeits his life? Or what shall a man give in return for his life? For the Son of man is to come with his angels in the glory of his Father (cf. Daniel), and then he will repay every man for what he has done. Truly, I say to you, there are some standing here who will not taste death before they see the Son of man coming in his kingdom" (Matthew 16:24-28).

Here appear the Passion and the scandal of the Cross.

We well know, through the experience of prayer and faith, that we are never finished with being convinced by God, instructed by him as to the depth of this mystery and at the same time, like the disciples, with repeatedly running away from it. No one can pronounce the final word on the mystery and scandal of the Cross until God has brought the mystery to its completion. It is not only a problem of understanding an event as if we were spectators, but it is the mystery of our own life which is present in Christ's Passion. Hence, whatever is said about it always falls short of what we have yet to experience and of what God will lead us to discover.

Yet this mystery of the Passion is the central mystery of Israel's faithfulness, because it is the problem of evil, of death, of the suffering of the righteous and God's goodness, of God's faithfulness, and of God who gives and sustains life. It is truly the intolerable mystery. The Psalms are filled with it.

We must confront this mystery when we would rather have God do justice, that is, root out evil. God seems to remain silent and fail to accomplish what man, his righteous one, asks of him. But what just person can utter these words: "I have done no evil, I have been faithful to your Covenant . . . ," if not Jesus, the Righteous One? And who other than he can ask that God's omnipotence reign, that is, ask for the coming of the ultimate Day of Judgment when evil will be vanquished and good will triumph, when God's goodness will be stronger and more manifest than all the powers of death? Faced with this mystery of evil and death, Israel stumbles and God must come to the rescue in the figure of obedient Israel. But Jesus also seems to stumble: "You are a hindrance to me." Jesus, faced with Peter's wish to avoid the outcome, experiences the same combat as the one evoked at the time of the temptations in the wilderness.

He overcomes this temptation by asking the disciples who have been given to him by the Father, his Assembly, to accompany him to Jerusalem, to share in his death, his ordeal. It is through his disciples that he overcomes the scandal of death, while at the same time giving them the strength to do it by taking them with him on his path. He calls them to come after him, to carry his cross and follow him.

The reasoning that follows — "What shall a man give in return for his life? Nothing" — pushes, in its absolute radicality, the disciple of Christ to choose God, just as Israel was called to choose him in the wilderness. It is this pressing question which recurs through the Gospel from beginning to end, and which sums up the Son's obedience. The choice whether to save one's life or lose it comes down to asking: from whom do I receive life? The act of faith consists of receiving one's life from God and from him alone. It is to let the source of life triumph in man, rather than to kill man. When heard by pagans who do not share Israel's hope, these words are given a murderous connotation, full of self-immolation and perversity, as if they conveyed that which is worst in us: an instinct for death or self destruction! This interpretation is a temptation for us. In reality, the act of faith overcomes this temptation of self-destruction in relying completely on God, who alone gives life in fullness. One does not search for life where there is death, but, on the contrary, we receive it where there is life. This act of faith is pushed to the point of paradox in faithfulness to life, to God's power, which is capable of entering into death. This is the contradiction before which the Psalmist as well as the prophets shudder, and yet continue to hope that God will resolve this paradox. Remember Isaiah's words: "The LORD of hosts will make for all peoples a feast of fat things . . ." (Isaiah 25:6).

This hope of life given by God is truly at the heart of Israel. In this respect the Pharisees are more faithful to Israel's hope than the Sadducees, who have retained only the dead life of the nation's political body. The Pharisees keep alive the hope of a people who lives from God.

The Transfiguration

"And after six days Jesus took with him Peter and James and John his brother and led them up to a high mountain." This vision is given only to these three witnesses, and to none other. We were not on the high mountain, we only have the witness and the attestation of what happened there. The Gospel emphasizes that only Peter, James, and John were granted an anticipated vision of the Lord in his Glory, and that it is not given to the others. Saint John will make a similar comment on the vision of the Risen Christ: "Blessed are those who have not seen and yet believe" (John 20:29).

For us, Peter, James and John are witnesses and guarantors. For the moment, the vision is not given to us, for the time has not yet come for us to see the Son of Man in his glory. It would be an error to believe that the coming of the Kingdom of God has been fully realized. It is at hand, it has already begun, but the time has not yet come when God will be "everything to everyone" and the Son himself will deliver the Kingdom to the Father.[7] This is not yet the time when all tears will be wiped away.[8] This is not yet the time when death will be vanquished; although it is already vanquished in the Son and, in a certain way, in us.[9] Yet we see clearly that we are still subject to death. Moreover, it is for this reason that, baptized in the death and resurrection of Christ, we can and we must, in him, share in his Passion.

One of the optical errors to which our spiritual desire can lead is to project a poorly conceived eschatology on the present time of the Church. Such an error disfigures the Christian hope. It transforms Christian life into a myth or, on the contrary, into an unbearable tyr-

---

7. Cf. 1 Corinthians 15:28 and 15:24.
8. Cf. Revelation 21:4.
9. Cf. 1 Corinthians 15:26

anny. We then try, by human means, to transform Christian society into a representation of the kingdom of heaven, whereas it is often only its infernal caricature. But God gives us the strength to hope. The loss of eschatological hope as a part of our Christian consciousness is certainly a source of considerable impoverishment and of great temptation. It consists in believing that God's kingdom "has come," and in wanting to give ourselves, by human means, what depends on God alone. The present time remains an obscure time, of hope and faithfulness, but not yet the time of glory. Wanting to anticipate that day of glory makes the share we have been given in the Cross of Christ in this time all the more unbearable and absurd, and renders futile the Cross of Christ itself.

At the instant of the Transfiguration, the three privileged disciples tell us of Jesus' meeting with Moses and Elijah. As Saint Luke will specify (9:31), they speak of Jesus' imminent departure in Jerusalem. Here the figure of Moses is crucial because it marks the moment of fulfillment. It is beyond death that Moses enters the Promised Land — he does not enter it in his lifetime — just as the Promised Land into which Jesus is going to enter lies beyond the ordeal of the Cross. The symbolism here is extremely powerful. Jesus is the new Moses, the prophet promised in Deuteronomy 18, who will come and teach all things. In this exchange, Moses and Elijah announce this fulfillment which comes in Jesus. It is impossible to imagine what they say; their words are hidden from us, but their very presence suggests what they talk about: they speak of the reason for which they have been sent by God, and of what is necessary for us if we are to enter into this mystery.

The three disciples hear the voice of the Father who designates Jesus as the obedient Son; it is the same vision that was given at Jesus' baptism to him alone, and the order to "listen to him," since he is precisely the prophet and the Son.[10]

After the vision, there remains, for this time, none but "Jesus only."[11]

10. Cf. Matthew 17:5.
11. Cf. Matthew 17:8.

CHAPTER 8

Christ's Passion Reveals the Sin of All

L et us now approach the end of Saint Matthew's Gospel beginning with chapter 26, the account of the Passion.

While the grace God can give us through such words is immeasurable, I would like to point out several aspects which can help us to understand the mystery of the Church as it is given to us and, consequently, the mystery of Election and the way in which God guides all events.

In this narrative, as in those of the other three evangelists, we are struck by the fact that Christ's Passion reveals the sin of all. This fact is truly underlined, with meticulous, systematic insistence, in the story told by the evangelists, as in the way the events unfolded, and in which Jesus wished them to unfold.

This universal revelation of sin is a capital point for discovering the meaning of this mystery, which will remain incomprehensible to the disciples: that "it was necessary that the Son of Man should be handed over and die" before entering "into his glory," according to the response that the as yet unknown companion on the road gives to the two disciples walking toward Emmaus (cf. Luke 24:26). This failure to understand that the "Son of Man" has to suffer to enter into his glory is the central mystery of the Messiah, of whom we are the disciples. It is the mystery that remains veiled and hidden until the end of time.

The Passion: Our Sin

Christ's Passion serves to reveal the sin of each and all. I begin by listing the various protagonists.

There are the chief priests and the scribes. There are the rulers of the people who reverse their judgment: they impugn Jesus, who himself appears as the high priest of Israel.

There are the people, who act rashly and who prophesy, sealing in spite of itself the New Covenant in the blood of the Lamb. The phrase, "His blood be on us and on our children," often understood — which is absurd — as a self-accusation, is a prophetic statement.[1] It recalls the moment when, at the foot of Mount Sinai, Moses sealed the Covenant between God and his people by sprinkling on the people the blood of the offerings (Exodus 24:8). It is, prophetically, a sign of forgiveness and benediction. It really requires a imagination totally devoid of faith to see in it a reprobation. To do so is to understand nothing of the meaning of the blood of the Covenant. Could the blood of the Covenant condemn, when it is spilt to save? To think so would be to refuse to believe in the Savior. The people, prophesying in spite of themselves — like Caiaphas, as Saint John says — prefer Jesus-Barabbas, Jesus "son of nobody," to Jesus the Christ, the Messiah.

There are the leaders. There are the people. There are the pagans. They all deny responsibility. They all reverse their decisions. Rome claims to be the representative of justice — justice based on reason — and to be the guarantor of respect for order. But, in this case, Rome's justice is transformed into a denial of justice, into a refusal to judge and the avoidance of responsibility. And flight from responsibility is not the least of sins. But, paradoxically, it is the pagans who designate Jesus as king of the Jews, which he remains forever, in spite of all temptations to co-opt him or forget this fundamental fact. Our crucifixes still bear, most of the time, the title which, as Saint John specifies, was written in Hebrew, Latin, and Greek at the head of the cross: "Jesus of Naza-

---

1. Cf. Matthew 27:25.

reth, King of the Jews."[2] This title designates, from the pagans' point of view, not the king "of Israel," but the king "of the Jews," to emphasize that which was the most ethnic and contemptible aspect in the Romans' eyes. He whom the disciples recognize as universal Lord is so only to the extent that his disciples, Jews and non-Jews alike, accept that he is the king of the Jews.

There is a last group: the disciples and apostles who betray, and betray as was predicted, announced, as if already taken up in God's forgiveness, Christ's forgiveness. Saint Matthew reports: "Jesus said to them, 'You will all fall away because of me this night; for it is written, "I will strike the shepherd, and the sheep of the flock will be scattered" (Zechariah). But after I am raised up, I will go before you to Galilee.'" To which Peter replies: "Though they all fall away because of you, I will never fall away." Jesus' answers: "Truly, I say to you, this very night before the cock crows, you will deny me three times." Peter insists: "Even if I must die with you, I will not deny you." And so say all the disciples (Matthew 26:31-35).

The Evangelist thus emphasizes that Christ's Passion reveals the sins of all, including those who will be the Church, the disciples given to Jesus by the Father.

The Passion: Our Forgiveness

This does not mean, however, that the guilt is equally shared. There is rather a divine intention that we must come to understand. There is a spiritual necessity, derived from the very nature of salvation which requires that the sin of all be revealed, including that of Jesus' followers. In other words, it is neither accidental nor an unfortunate happenstance, due to a particular cowardice or to a momentary lack of courage; it is tied to the very superabundance of the redemptive act.

Christ, because he is the Innocent One, is totally obedient to God. By his very innocence and obedience to God, he unmasks the homi-

2. Cf. John 19:19-22.

cidal tendency which is in the heart of every man. He unmasks it in accepting to become its victim.

Sin is a kind of war, a case of man setting himself up against God. The innocence and righteousness of the Son — Word made flesh, Son of God made man — bring to light the homicidal tendency which dwells in the heart of every man.

Sin is thus revealed by the innocence of the only Innocent One. Because he is innocent, displaying the fullness of righteousness and submission, sin is revealed by the contrast in its true nature. By accepting to receive this wound, the Innocent One reveals the wound hidden in the secret of human hearts. In Christ's wounds, man can see himself as he is: not in another sinner, but in the Innocent One whom he disfigures. Adam, Man, can contemplate himself in Christ, for in the wounds he inflicts on the Innocent, the Righteous One, he sees his own portrait. In the derision he heaps upon Jesus, he sees his own blasphemous thoughts. In the blows he gives him, he sees his own cruelty. In the apostles' betrayal, he sees his own cowardice. In Jesus abandoned, he sees his own abandonment of God.

Paul will say: "For our sake he made him to be sin" (2 Corinthians 5:21). He is the one who reveals man's sin by accepting to bear it, for man's sin is always ultimately turned against the greatness and goodness of God, of which man is the sacrament. Only the holiness of the obedient Son reveals the refusal that dwells in every man's heart; and if he permits sin to be thus revealed, it is in order to make universal forgiveness possible.

In the Passion, all of humanity is represented; it is present in all possible categories, according to the symbolism of Scripture: both Jews and pagans, hence all mankind, participate in the Passion. These are the great categories of human society in Scripture. All see their own sin revealed, so that all can be forgiven by God and all can receive mercy.

Forgiveness is indeed given to all: to the people by the blood cast on it; to the pagans who recognize Jesus as "a righteous man" and "Son of God"; to the apostles through the mercy that Christ grants them; to the chief priest through the promise of the vision of the "Son of Man." To all the hope of forgiveness is given, and to this end the sin of all is revealed.

Our sin must be measured by Christ's Passion for us to be able to receive God's forgiveness. For it is only in Christ's Passion, and in contemplating him, that we can discover our sin not in despair or damnation, but in God's forgiveness.

If our sin had been revealed elsewhere than at the Cross, we would not have received forgiveness; Hell would have seized us. Man would not have been able to see his sin without dying, because then he would see God's justice, which would have, literally, pulverized him. His sin would be unbearable. He would have locked himself into a suicidal reality of death or damnation, which amount to the same. Whereas, at the Cross, our sin becomes accessible because it is given to us to see it in the sacrifice made for us by the Righteous One, "betrayed into the hands of sinners," in the words of Saint Matthew.[3] Mercy is granted to us. The Son is delivered into the hands of sinners by the Father: it is the Father who gives up his Son to them, and who thus shows his love.

The evangelist shows this clearly in his description of the arrest of Jesus. Peter and the others intervene, and want to use force. Jesus says to him, "Put your sword back into its place; for all who take the sword will perish by the sword. Do you think that I cannot appeal to my Father, and he will at once send me more than twelve legions of angels? But how then should the scriptures be fulfilled, that it must be so?" (Matthew 26:52-54).

And Saint Matthew repeats: "'All this has taken place, that the scriptures of the prophets might be fulfilled.' Then all the disciples forsook him and fled" (Matthew 26:56).

Therefore, Jesus is given up by the Father to the homicidal instinct of men. Not because the Father is an executioner, but because of his compassion for those he has created — for Israel and for all humanity. The Father delivers the Son into the hands of sinners in order to reveal the sins of mankind and to grant them forgiveness.

3. Cf. Matthew 26:45.

At the same time that he offers us mercy, Jesus leads us to measure the perfection of his gift of self, as the obedient Son, since he submits himself unceasingly to the Father. Trusting in the One who is the source of life, he obeys his holy will and commandments to the extreme point of death. In doing so, he opens the way to the Resurrection; he reveals the power of God's reign, which comes through the Son's obedience, through his perfect accomplishment of the commandments.

The Resurrection is indeed the result of Jesus' obedience because, trusting in his Father even unto death, Jesus leads the way to life stronger than death. He breaks open the gates of death that are linked to sin. Thus, his disciples are given the anticipation of the resurrected life in Christ. Christ is the one who enters into life through his perfect obedience to the Father, and he "gives up the Spirit," not only in the sense of "expiring," but so that this Spirit can in turn be given to men.[4] Henceforth, the disciples are granted a glimpse of the resurrected life, and also share in Christ's obedience. They in turn will receive the Spirit given up by Jesus as a sharing in his obedience. Thus, they are offered the possibility of living in perfect, loving submission to the Father, by receiving forgiveness, by seeing their sins revealed and forgiven, and by their participation in the act by which Jesus himself accomplishes this deliverance and this salvation.

This giving up of the Spirit is thus the opening, at the moment of Jesus' utter solitude, of the new way; the opening of the way to life as it has been promised and as the disciples will receive it, in the gift freely given to them by Christ, by the Father.

The Passion: The Road to Life

The death of Christ simultaneously reveals sin, lets us measure the depth of our sin, makes forgiveness possible, and opens the road to life. For there to be forgiveness, sin must be revealed. There is a close parallel to be drawn between the Law and Christ. Since it is God's holy

4. Cf. John 19:30.

will, the Law also reveals man's sin, but instead of delivering the sinner, it makes him aware of his own powerlessness.

When the Law is loved and obeyed by the obedient Son to the point of identifying himself with this holy will, with this holy law, fulfilling it to perfection, then sin is unveiled: "For our sake he made him to be sin who knew no sin" (2 Corinthians 5:21).

The Cross might have been our condemnation, but mercy is granted to us through Jesus' obedience. God himself, in giving us his Son who perfectly accomplishes his holy will in love and submission, delivers us from the condemnation we would have pronounced on ourselves if we had been imprisoned in our incapacity to obey, if we could see only the extent of our flight, our refusal.

God grants us a double gift of grace by giving us his holy will and in bridging the gap revealed by this will between him and us: the distance of our sin. It is this abyss that the Son crosses, the abyss of death from which he emerges to open the door to life.

Saint Matthew shows how God already gives the Resurrection to his obedient Son. The Church will add: also to Mary. Yet the evangelist specifies: "And behold, the curtain of the temple was torn in two, from top to bottom; and the earth shook, and the rocks were split; the tombs also were opened, and many bodies of the saints who had fallen asleep were raised, and coming out of the tombs after his resurrection they went into the holy city and appeared to many" (Matthew 27:51-53).

This tells us that all the righteous of the Covenant are raised from the dead, and enter into the resurrection, at the moment of Christ's death.

This is a passage that we often avoid, or fail to understand, because it seems to us to be strange, incredible. And yet, it conveys a central point of the Christian faith, which is that the first-fruits of the Resurrection are thus given to the righteous, in the experience of the Spirit, given after Christ's death.

The Passion: Our Vocation

Christ's Passion is the crucial moment of our destiny, since in it we see not only our sin, our forgiveness, our life, but, in a certain sense, also our vocation as disciples who are called to participate in the mission of the suffering Messiah, following Mary's example. This vocation, understood in strictly human terms, would be unbearable and unacceptable. We can join in this messianic work only on the condition that we receive the light and strength to do so as a grace from God. It is precisely this grace of life that is given to believers.

To recognize why Christ had to suffer before entering into his glory is to cease being scandalized by this mystery of evil — not because we finally understand it, but because God in his mercy leads us into it, takes us by the hand when we are tempted to run away, and leaves us there in great peace, showing us, at least, the fruits of joy and glory that are our hope and of which we are the guarantors.

Even if the faith of Jesus' disciples constantly wavers on this central point, even if our sin and weakness lead each of us to retreat, the specifically Christian grace, the grace given to Christ's disciple, is not only to receive the fulfillment of that for which Israel still hopes, but also to receive the strength to remain with Christ at this point, and to share, as a grace of forgiveness and peace, his mission as the crucified servant whom God brings to life. From a human point of view, this grace is unbelievable, unbearable. It remains a "stumbling block" and a "folly" in our eyes, even if we are daily immersed in it, if only by the sacrament of the Eucharist.[5]

We know what peace and joy are given to us there. Here is that to which we must constantly bear witness: forgiveness incessantly received and, through it, life incessantly restored. Prayer must constantly bring us back to this. In any case, it makes us realize the extent of our sin. We cannot pray without perceiving our distance from God, if only by the content of our prayer, if only by the distractions and unmasking of our cowardice, which are only the normal effects of prayer. By keep-

5. Cf. 1 Corinthians 1:23.

ing us close to him, God mercifully allows us to see just how much we have distanced ourselves from him. It pleases him to give us the first-fruits of his Son's saving act, in which he allows us to participate. The Spirit of Jesus, which was yielded up to the Father, is poured out on us and grants us the strength to experience this death, and to experience it as a source of life. We become what we receive, since we receive a crucified and resurrected Christ. We become the one who comes to dwell in us. We become his body, we live of his Spirit. If we were to imagine that we can live this mystery by our own strength, we would behave no differently than the disciples, who, at the moment of the Lord's Passion, ran away . . .

CHAPTER 9

Jesus Crucified, the Messiah of Israel: Salvation for All

L et us pause at this point in the Gospel, facing the Crucified Christ, facing the Risen Christ, because it is a single mystery. This is the precise point where we become Christians. There is no other entry to the Christian condition; there is no other way to participate in Christ, since it is through this act of fulfillment that the grace of salvation and Israel's Election are offered to us, to Christians.

Let us consider this point yet further, as we reflect once again on the mystery of Israel. We cannot claim to substitute our reflection on Israel for Israel's own. We must reflect on ourselves, on our position in regard to this mystery. That does not mean simply being intrigued by a strange or alien reality, by the singularity of the Jews' fate in history. Such reflection might lead to an outpouring of pity; it would certainly exclude us from a mystery which concerns us, if we are of Christ. For the mystery of Israel is inseparably the mystery of Christ's disciples. This truth is exactly what we are tempted to refuse, what we are constantly refusing. By that refusal, the mystery of Israel becomes foreign to the faith of Christians. When this happens, any Christian discourse on Israel risks becoming intolerable for Israel. However, the objective of our reflection is not to be tolerable or intolerable to Jews, but be faithful to the truth of that which God asks of us. We must understand that we are dealing with a Christian mystery, a fundamentally Christian mystery. It touches perhaps the most sensitive point of our faith, since it is our very faithfulness to God that is at stake.

This is not a question for open debate. It is the central mystery which shapes the Christian faith. To make of Israel only a particular case, and, ultimately, an ethnic case — which it is also in certain respects — is a temptation for the Christian. We yield to this temptation if we consider the Jewish population as we would any other: there are some countries without Jews, others where there are many; there are countries which have tried to solve the Jewish question by expulsion, others by murder. That the Jewish question has been localized, relativized in this way only makes it all the more crucial for the world and for the Jews themselves. But the mystery of Israel remains at the center of the Christian faith. If we consider it unessential, we expose just how far we are from being Christians.

This point is much more important than it appears. Even though the centrality of this mystery is not denied theoretically, it is in practice. This denial is the Marcionite temptation.[1] Marcion was a heretic in the early days of the Church who wished to eliminate the Old Testament from the New. This rejection of the Old Testament has been a permanent temptation, which the Church has rejected as an attack on her own faith. Nevertheless, Marcionism remains latently present in all generations.

Today, the great pagan civilizations such as India remain alien to the Judeo-Christian West. There is currently a Christian theological movement that claims that the scriptures of India are its "Old Testament." That amounts to saying that the Old Testament's only role is that of a cultural substratum in regard to the New Testament. In that case, should we then say that the archaic and animist African culture is the Old Testament of Africa?

The question is to understand how it is that educated, honest, sin-

---

1. Marcion (A.D. 85-160) was a Gnostic heretic from Sinope on the Black Sea. Excommunicated in Rome in A.D. 144, he founded the Marcionite Church, which spread in the Mediterranean Basin and Mesopotamia and remained influential until around 400. Marcion's *Antitheses* are known through the writings of his adversaries (Tertullian, Theophilus of Antioch). His thought is a radical Paulinism, which reduces the Scriptures to Luke's Gospel and Paul's letters.

cere Christians can be led to a rejection of their roots in the Old Testament. We have here a test which touches the very heart of faith. Such a temptation is the subject of a spiritual combat that requires of us a choice in regard to God, and so supposes that we offer up our lives. We can only give our consent through the usual means of a choice made in the Holy Spirit, prayer, and union with the Crucified.

It is not a matter of taking sides and adding to the world's cacophony. But to perceive these stakes, when we are consecrated to God, requires us to immerse ourselves yet more deeply in the offering made of our lives in order to overcome this test.

The Church needs all this gathered spiritual force to surmount such a test, which is a real temptation. This kind of temptation, "this kind of demon," can be chased away, not by disciplinary measures, but by an abundance of freedom, of love, and of offering of ourselves — hence, by prayer.

In this combat, the most hidden, the most deeply buried, the most unknown of all prayer is needed for the Church to be able to welcome God's choice, recognize it, and respond to it faithfully.

A Mystery within Christianity

Let us go yet deeper into this mystery, which becomes accessible only if we allow the Gospel to lead us to the point where we stand facing Christ, the crucified Messiah of Israel, rejected by all and yet opening the way of salvation to all.

We contemplate Christ on the Cross, the obedient and living Son, the Son who obeys up to the moment of death, giving himself up entirely to God with absolute and pure faithfulness, and receiving from the Father the Resurrection promised to Israel, faithful to the Law. His Resurrection is the logical result of his yielding up his life to God, the source of life. In the obedient and risen Son, we see Israel's fulfillment, which does not mean its abolition or annihilation. Israel's fulfillment has yet to be received by Israel itself. That is a problem to be faced by Israel, and also God's secret.

God chooses, among all the pagan nations, sons and daughters who, through faith in Christ, the obedient and risen Son, the plenitude of Israel, henceforth share in Israel's Election, grace, and mission. With the Christ-Messiah and through him, pagans who were not a people, who were without Law, without hope or recourse, who did not know God — receive the grace of entering into Israel's Election.[2] This is the Christian vocation. It is, through and with the crucified and living Messiah, to share in the filial adoption promised to Israel.

Furthermore, the theory that Israel has been rejected is shown to be senseless, an absurdity, because it implies that God could be unfaithful to his Covenant. It is to misunderstand the mystery of Christ himself. For the Son, by his Passion, in his obedience, bestows the Spirit, promised to Israel, and pours it out on the pagans as well. He makes it possible for those who are his to observe truly, if still in hope, the Covenant in the Spirit, where the Law is inscribed in the hearts of God's children. The Messiah first realizes in himself the prophetic promise, the hope of Deuteronomy, and he enables his disciples, still confronted with sin and death, to participate in his life.

Christian baptism is the baptism received by Jesus from John the Baptist. Through it, pagans are received into the people of Israel. Jesus subjected himself to this rite so as to be obedient to God, as Israel is called to be obedient to God, and he lives this baptism to the very end. Referring to his Passion, Jesus said to his disciples, "I have a baptism to be baptized with; and how I am constrained until it is accomplished."[3] This baptism of the New Covenant is accomplished by Christ in his death when which he pours out the Spirit that descended on him at the moment of his baptism by John in the Jordan. When those who become his family, "his brothers and sisters," receive this same baptism, they have, by him, a share in the hope of Israel. The Christians baptized in the Messiah share in the mystery accomplished by Jesus' baptism. They share in the promises, according to the prophetic expressions, and particularly those found in Hosea (1:9; 2:1-3, 25) and repeated in the

---

2. Cf. Ephesians 2:12; Romans 2:14.
3. Cf. Luke 12:50.

New Testament: "You who were not my people will be called my people," etc. (cf. Revelation 21:3; 2 Corinthians 6:16).

"They Shall Be My People"

The expression "people of God," which has flourished since the Council of Vatican II used it in *Lumen Gentium*, is presently subject to considerable abuse. A close inspection reveals that the people of God is only mentioned three times in the New Testament: once in the First Letter of Peter (2:10), and twice in the Letter to the Hebrews (4:9 and 11:25). In two of the three cases, it refers to the people of Israel. In the third, the first quotation from the Letter to the Hebrews, it designates the people of Israel as an eschatological people; the context is the Sabbath, apropos of Joshua, and of the expression: "they shall not enter my rest."

In the New Testament letters, there are frequent references to the people that God has acquired for his own, but the term is always used in a very precise sense. It is the "redeemed" people, but that means the people redeemed from Egypt. It is the people of Israel to whom God has given the grace of having new sons and daughters; or else it is Isaiah's announcement that pagans will be joined to Israel: "You were not of the people; now you are, you are the people God has acquired for himself."[4] There is no substitution, but on the contrary, an incorporation of pagans into the people which depends entirely on God and which, in its obedience to God, receives all its sustenance from him.

Today, the word *people* has a political connotation which suggests just the inverse. The "sovereign people" acts not according to God's wishes, but its own. This is one of the major temptations of the people of Israel, and is also one of the forms of pagan regression exhibited by Christians. We see this very clearly in the Bible.[5] The people want to control their own destiny, to be a people like the others, masters of their fate, their leaders, their gods, their kings, etc, whereas the whole

4. Cf. Isaiah 54:1-3; 55:5.
5. Cf. 1 Samuel 8:5-22; Ezekiel 20:32.

act of faith is to relinquish this control. At the price of taking what seems to be a mortal risk, the people must rely entirely on God, and on him alone, even in the most critical periods of the kingdom.

This is the essence of the test of faith. The people are constituted as a people only to the extent that they accept renouncing their own control. And this will reach the absolute paradox where the people will be deprived of their kings and their Temple and, at the moment when Christ, the Messiah, arrives, will have entered into a period of an almost complete expropriation of their earthly destiny.

Through faith in Christ, the obedient and resurrected Son, the fulfillment of Israel, sons and daughters will come from all nations and have access to the Election, the grace, and the mission of Israel.

The Sign of Jonah

The next step is to let all the consequences of this grace unfold, to discover our image given in Christ, because it is only in and through Christ, by having a share in the Messiah and the gift of the Spirit that we can enter into the Covenant and the Election. That is our place; that is the point where the Church of the Resurrected is born.

Through faith in Christ and the gift of the Spirit, the pagans turn away from their idols. At least, that is what has been promised to Israel, and that Israel has never seen, because this hope that the pagans will turn away from their idols always seems blocked. Yet the hope of their conversion remains: "Those who were lost in the land of Assyria and those who were driven out to the land of Egypt will come and worship the LORD" (Isaiah 27:13; cf. Psalm 67:32). Remember what was said of Cyrus (Ezra 1; Isaiah 44:28 and 45). On the day of the Lord, paganism will give way before the living God. References to this day are often found in the Psalms: "The Lord is the Lord of all the earth."[6] These assertions are not the megalomania of a people who are making their God into the universal God. They are the hope, at the very heart of Is-

---

6. For example, cf. Psalms 83:18; 95:3; 97:9.

rael's own existence and faithfulness — Israel, too, had to be delivered from idols forged by man — that this deliverance will be given to all and that the pagans will come to recognize the true and living God, the One God, God of all the earth, the eternal God.

This hope was never realized in biblical times. Hence, it remains an eschatological hope for the end of time — among those yet to be accomplished: in one way or another, all the pagan nations will emerge from their paganism or idolatry and recognize the true and living God. In Christ, even if as yet incompletely, we see the beginnings, the first-fruits, of this abandonment of idols for the worship of the unique God — the God of Abraham, Isaac, and Jacob.

This too is a sign given to Israel. It is the meaning, for example, of the sign of Jonah, as presented by Saint Luke: "This generation . . . seeks a sign, but no sign shall be given to it except the sign of Jonah" (Luke 11:29-32). In Saint Matthew's Gospel, this sign is that of the whale, of the symbolism of death and resurrection (Matthew 12:38-42). But the same sign is seen by Saint Luke from the angle of the pagans who repent and are converted to the living God. It is a sign that the coming of the Messiah is at hand or that he has already come.

We have to ask ourselves — and this is where humble supplication before God is crucial — if the peoples who have been led to turn away from their idols have truly abandoned their gods, just how far their combat against idols has progressed, and who can claim that the name of Christian designates those who serve the true God. We can only raise such a question if we feel its pain within us, not as an accusation. The point is not to accuse — that would lead nowhere — but to take upon ourselves what we recognize as a sin and, if God grants us that grace, to pray that this sin be forgiven, that the strength to renounce it will emerge. But it is plain to see that under the cover of faithfulness to the Covenant and belonging to the Covenant, the figure of Christ has often served as a pretext to forget the Father, the unique God. One of the tragedies of Christian civilization is that it has become atheistic while claiming to remain Christian. It has made Christ into an idolatrous figure, a son without a father — and thus without the Spirit; its only spirit, ultimately, is the spirit of man.

As a result, the figure of Christ becomes a cultural absolute, and a perverted, blasphemous messianism finds there its justification. We should not rejoice that Jesus has become "fashionable," because there is no worse idol than that which imitates the true God.

This idolatry has taken many historical forms across the centuries. There is no point in enumerating them. But today, it bears specific names: "atheistic Christianity" is proposed as a possible alternative to the Church. It is undoubtedly one of the contemporary temptations. The remedy is not a vigorous hierarchy that would reestablish sanctions and disciplines. This temptation must be exorcised from the inside. People do not turn away from idols by imperial decree. A converted Constantine was not sufficient to uproot the idols.[7] To uproot them, we must be converted in depth. It is a spiritual combat.

The Holiness Promised to Israel

Through faith in Christ and the gift of the Spirit, the pagans have access to the plenitude of holiness promised to Israel. This holiness reveals the holiness of God; it is the sign in this world of his joy and of the hope of a new world. This is the whole meaning of the Covenant with its precepts and commandments: "be holy, for I the LORD am holy" (Leviticus 20:26; 1 Peter 1:16); "You, therefore, must be perfect, as your heavenly Father is perfect" (Matthew 5:48). Thus, through the gift of the Holy Spirit which is given to us in the New Covenant, the Father reveals himself as a light in our works. And the pagan nations will see God's glory in his power acting in us, in his holiness working within us.

This is Israel's vocation, in which the pagans share through Christ. They have a right to the holiness promised to Israel through Christ who gives the Spirit and makes this holiness possible.

If the previous temptation concerned idols — the temptation of

---

7. Constantine I, the Great, was Roman Emperor from 306 to 337. The son of Saint Helen, he guaranteed freedom to Christians by the Edicts of Milan in 313, a step that was equivalent to recognizing Christianity as the state religion.

the Baals and of Canaan[8] — we can say that here another pagan temptation appears: the temptation of Sodom, of corruption of the received revelation.[9] Here too, we must examine our consciences regarding the way the pagan peoples, who received Christianity as an historical and cultural heritage, have reacted to their entry into the Covenant. To what extent can we today claim to be Christians when we continue to live like pagans? Instead of letting the purity and holiness of God shine forth in us, we are often worse than the pagans. We often show the face of Satan, the Tempter, under the mask of "death," "power," and "blasphemy."

It would be an error to blame the state of civilization for this. A "Christian empire" cannot be created by the patrols of a vice squad. The problem is spiritual. The true nature of the combat for holiness depends on grace and faithfulness to the Holy Spirit. So, in this time of history in which we live, prior to the coming of the glorious reign, we are still locked into this combat in which the gift of self, forgiveness, the miracle of grace, and the power of the Holy Spirit are all intertwined.

To this should bear witness the pagans and Jews who have received the gift of the Spirit from the Messiah. They should thus strive to outdo each other in holiness and love, in consecration to God and purity of life. "For I tell you, unless your righteousness exceeds that of the scribes and Pharisees, you will never enter the kingdom of heaven" (Matthew 5:20). It is all there, in black and white, in the Gospel. But we have understood nothing of the Gospel if we deduce from this that the scribes and Pharisees are hypocrites, and that we are better; our holiness must surpass even that, already very demanding, of the scribes and Pharisees, and this holiness must be entirely given by the force of the Holy Spirit.

8. Baal, the god of wind and rain, was the most important of the Canaanite fertility gods. The most detailed of the biblical references to this god is the duel of the prophet Elijah with the 450 prophets of Baal gathered at Mount Carmel; cf. 1 Kings 18:19-40. Eventually, the name "Baal" was given to all the pagan divinities. The prophets constantly denounced this idolatry; see, for example, Hosea 2:15, 19; Jeremiah 7:9; 9:13.

9. Cf. Genesis 14:21-24; Ezekiel 16:48-49.

In the eighteenth century, at the beginning of the modern era, the faithfulness to God within Judaism brought about, in Central and Eastern Europe, an extraordinary mystical movement: Hassidism.[10] It goes as far as is imaginable for the rabbinical culture in the expectation of the Messiah's coming in this time of suffering. What comparable figure of holiness could be found at the same period among the pagan-Christian peoples, where atheism was already being born out of modernity? The peoples of this world, the nations, the historical periods, the generations have a responsibility in faith. Faith shapes a people, creates a social existence lived in holiness and love.

In our time of history, it not our task to exhort Israel, but, in letting God act within us, to give Israel a perceptible sign of the grace thus given to it. There is a double sign, mutually given by each to the other: the pagans must recognize in Jesus the grace given to Israel, because they share in that grace; and Israel must welcome the hope manifested by the wonders that God accomplishes among the pagans. Thus, each group bears witness to the other that it is an unearned gift that it has received. It is this mutual recognition, this freely given reciprocity that is the object of our hope. But for this to happen, the pagans must fulfill their vocation of bearing witness to the fact that they share in God's gift to Israel.

When pagans reverse the mystery by killing Israel in the name of a faith perverted by paganism, the Messiah becomes unrecognizable. How can Israel possibly recognize its Messiah in the figure that is presented to it? Israel can see in it only sin, death, horror, the devil, and Satan.

But mutual acknowledgment is broadly announced in Scripture, in particular by Saint Paul.[11] We see it also in certain parables quoted

---

10. Hassidism grew out of a popular Jewish movement of religious revival. The sect was founded by Israel Ben Baal Sem Tov in the eighteenth century in Podolia, a part of Ukraine which had been under Polish rule since 1699, following the Treaty of Karlowitz. The members of this sect pursued the ideal of *hasidout* ("holiness") and joy in the service of God. See "Hassidisme," in *Dictionnaire encyclopédique du judaïsme* (Paris: Cerf, 1993), pp. 486-501.

11. Cf. Romans 11.

by Saint Luke. For example, the parable of the two sons: the elder (Israel) and the younger (the son who goes to live with the pagans, far from his father's home, and ends up eating with the swine).[12]

The younger son who returns home should be a sign for the older one. But, of course, for that to be so the younger one must say: "I have sinned, Father." Only then does he receive an superabundance of grace, and this grace should be for the elder a sign of the superabundant grace which is given to him, too: "Son, you are always with me." The logic of this superabundance that God sets in motion in sacred history is all there, pointed out simply, clearly, naively.

12. Cf. Luke 15:11-32; this parable is usually referred to as the "Parable of the Prodigal Son."

CHAPTER 10

Access through Christ to All the Riches of Israel

L et us continue with what might be called a litany: the enumeration of the riches to which God gives us access through the Cross of his Christ. Once we have started to make an inventory, we discover that these riches are inexhaustible.

These riches are those that have already been received by Israel. In Christ they are offered to both Jews and pagans, as a grace, in a radically new way.

It is normal that a disciple of Christ should discover these riches from a new perspective: he recognizes in them a fulfillment and a novelty that would have been inaccessible to him if he had not believed that Jesus is the Messiah.

Admittedly, this understanding in Christ does not coincide with the way the Jew who does not recognize Christ as the Messiah perceives his own riches. Nevertheless, the vision he has of himself is not outdated, nor meaningless. This radical difference in interpretation stems precisely from the mystery of Christ himself, who gives pagans access to Israel's riches and gives Israel a new light on its mystery, at the price of his blood. The Jew who accedes to the mystery of Christ receives this light. We must return to this point and to its possible consequences for mutual acceptance as well as for the Church's present attitude. But, for the pagan granted access to Israel's riches, it is first of all a discovery, a prayer of thanks for the goodness of God, who freely gives an unearned gift.

Sacred History

Through faith in Christ, the obedient and risen Son, the fulfillment of Israel, pagans called from among all the nations now have access to Israel's history. They who were without a past, without a history, without a Covenant, receive the revelation of history as revealed by God to his people, a sacred history (cf. Romans and Ephesians). Obviously, the word *history* is not to be understood here in the critical sense, but as the founding gesture of God, which gives human life its meaning.

Where there is no Election, there is no history. This is easy to verify in our personal lives. Our lives lose themselves in insignificance, in nothingness, in nostalgia for times past or a happiness that has disappeared; they are deprived of meaning as long as we do not receive them in the love of God, who chooses us and gives us a share in the Election. Only then do we realize how much we are loved and how God calls us, chooses us. Then our past is given back to us as a blessing. Even those events that appeared to be misfortunes or losses can suddenly be received as a source of joy and thanksgiving. Even our faults can be transformed by forgiveness — they are truly changed, and not because our memory has modified them. For then we bear our past in an entirely different way, as a result of the mercy that reconciles us with God and with ourselves.

This is what happens when the risen Lord invites his disciples to touch his wounds (Luke 24; John 20:27). He leads them to take a decisive step in faith. It was not a question of verifying his identity; his wounds are the reminder of their betrayal. The disciples had fled when faced with them, and this is why their memory remains wounded. Our own experience holds events which we have chosen to forget rather than face an unbearable past. Similarly, the pilgrims on the road to Emmaus cannot understand what they remember. Christ has to enlighten them by interpreting what they have seen only obscurely.

Then, he restores their memory of his life and their own by forgiving them for their abandonment. Through this forgiveness, he makes the Passion, from which they had fled, accessible to them. With memory restored to them, they receive their own lives, transfigured.

It is with the same hope of mercy that Israel can recall the whole history of the world, through the Election it receives. The pagans, too, now have access to this memory of the salvation of the multitude. This is why the Church, in celebrating the Messiah's Passover on Holy Saturday, commemorates the entire history of humanity, beginning with the story of creation.[1]

Thus, this motion of worship and thanksgiving leads us to bear the memory of all humanity by sharing Israel's memory. In Christ, the pagans have access to the sacred history of Israel, which becomes their history, and Abraham becomes their father: "God is able from these stones to raise up children to Abraham" (Matthew 3:9). In raising from the dead, in giving resurrected life, Christ fulfills this word. And those who were not sons have become sons.

The Law of God

Pagans also have a right to the Law, as a holy law inscribed in their hearts. It is by acting through the Messiah, with him and in him who made himself obedient to the Law to death on the Cross, that they obey the Law. The discipline of the Church dispenses them from Israel's observances, a burden too heavy for them, and which remains Israel's privilege.[2]

It is not for the pagans to take on the physical history of the Hebrews, since they, through Christ, have become spiritual offspring of Abraham, but not his physical descendants. Nevertheless, in Christ they have access to the plenitude of the Law, and receive the Holy Spirit

---

1. In the liturgy of Easter Eve, celebrated during the night of Holy Saturday, the Church proposes Genesis 1:1–2:4 as the first reading.

2. Cf. Acts of the Apostles 15:19:29.

which allows them to fulfill it. They can enter into the plenitude of holiness, into the complete fulfillment of the commandments, even if the observances of the Jewish condition are not imposed on them. That Jews refuse this distinction is easily understandable. But to refuse it in a Christian interpretation would be to revert to paganism. In fact, the mystery of Christ is the grace granted to pagans to keep the Law perfectly, to obey God's love, his holy will, and to enter into it in Christ's perfection and the freedom of the Holy Spirit.

Far from creating a disdain for the Law, this Christian interpretation should lead to an infinitely greater love for the Law, God's holy will, that is perfectly accomplished in Christ.

The Inspired Word

The pagans are also entitled to the inspired Word of God, the Bible. In this respect, the New Testament is considered Holy Scripture by Christians and it is indeed, but not in the same way as what we call the Old Testament; it is a part of the Church's living testimony on the mystery of Christ.

The Second Vatican Council's document "On the Revelation" (*Dei Verbum*) sheds light on the importance of Scripture in the Church's Tradition, especially with respect to the New Testament. What constitutes the New Testament is the mystery of Christ, first received in the life of the Church, in that living body which is the Body of Christ, in the sacraments celebrated by the Church. These writings are part of the living and present memory of the Church, of the Body of Christ.

This body then becomes capable of a Christian reading of the Old Testament. One does not draw on the ancient texts to have them say what we want them to say; they must be read in Christ, with the aid of the Holy Spirit. This kind of reading, in the condition of the Messiah, is one of the spiritual treasures of the past that are sometimes neglected nowadays.

Father de Lubac has brought out the fourfold sense of Scripture in his excellent book.[3] It is worth reading it in this perspective. There exists an abridged edition, very interesting for those who practice *lectio divina*: it can compensate for the sometimes overly dry aspects of a purely rationalist exegesis, in contrast with which rabbinical exegesis can appear absolutely sumptuous.[4] Only the patristic exegesis can be compared with it.

There is a Christian reading of the Bible. The New Testament leads us into the mystery of Christ; in him, through the force of the Holy Spirit, we receive the history of Israel; in him, it becomes our own. Far from being diminished, the Old Testament remains the place where the mystery of God, which we read in Christ, is revealed.

The Old and New Testaments cannot be read in the same way. They nourish the Christian in different ways. Moreover, this is why the Church has always very firmly maintained the place of the Old Testament in the liturgy — because there has been, and remains, a great temptation to reduce or eliminate it. Similarly, the liturgical proclamation of the Gospel is reserved to the priest or deacon.

Israel's Prayer

Pursuing my litany, I shall add that, through faith in Christ, pagans have access to Israel's prayer and, hence, to its mission to render glory to God.

Israel's form of worship was initially centered on the Temple. When the destruction of the Temple made this impossible, the rabbis and wise men, in particular the Pharisees, and the whole of Israel substituted the psalmic prayers, private or collective, which correspond

3. Henri de Lubac, *Exégèse médiévale* (Paris: Aubier, 1959). See also Henri de Lubac, "On an Old Distich: The Doctrine of the 'Fourfold Sense' in Scripture" in *Theological Fragments* (San Francisco: Ignatius Press, 1989), translated from *Théologies d'occasion* (Paris: Desclée de Brouwer, 1984).

4. *Écriture dans la Tradition* (Paris: Aubier-Montaigne, 1966). The *lectio divina* is the daily reading of passages of both the Old and the New Testament to nourish Christian prayer.

exactly to the prayers and sacrifices offered in the Temple. This is the structure of Jewish prayer, to which corresponds the monastic liturgy of the hours. Thus, by faith in Christ, the pagans have access to Israel's mission of prayer, including the use of the Psalms. They do not simply have access to the prayers — as they might have access to those of a pagan tradition, for example the *Bhagavad-Gita* — they also share in the mission to pray; they, too, are consecrated for prayer.[5] The way in which the Church accomplishes this mission is to pray, with Christ himself. The Christian who recites the Psalms does both for himself and in the name of the Church. When he says "I," the Church is speaking; it is also Christ himself who prays through his words.

To receive Christ's ongoing prayer in the Psalms prayed by the Church is one of the graces given through the Cross. It unites the pagan with Israel's prayer.

Similarly, through the Church's liturgy, pagans have access to the feasts of Israel. This is not simply an historical borrowing, which would link a certain celebration, such as Easter, to its chronological origin. The Christian feasts are the festivals of Israel celebrated by Jesus Christ and celebrated, in Christ, by his disciples. If this is forgotten, all understanding of them is lost. How can we understand the Eucharist and Easter, if we do not grasp that they are the Jewish Passover celebrated by Christ? This is no abusive drift. This is not the taking over of a pagan celebration to transform it into pious processions for the evangelization of a people, as was widely practiced. The Christian celebrations are fundamentally the feasts of Israel as they are experienced in and through Christ. That is the actual origin of our celebrations, and their historical source. This is the very nature of the Christian liturgy.

This Jewish origin of the Eucharist is also true for all the major Christian feasts. How can the feast of Easter be understood without realizing that it is the Passover of Israel celebrated by Christ? The same is

5. *Bhagavad-Gita,* or "The Song of the Lord," is a Sanskrit poem that is fundamental for Hindu philosophy. In it, the god Krishna explains to Arjuna the principles of action. The *Bhagavad-Gita* can be understood only within the context of the vast epic of the *Mahabharata.*

true for Pentecost: it is Israel's Pentecost, celebrated with the Assembly of Jesus.

We must not go too far, however, in seeking similarities and comparisons, for two thousand years as well as considerable cultural differences separate the celebrations. Nevertheless, a fundamental intuition makes it possible to understand that these are a single form of worship. Christians will go much further. They feel justified in saying that they are continuing the service of God in the "spiritual temple" they form. This was said by Saint Paul, and again by Saint Peter: "Like living stones be yourselves built into a spiritual house, to be a holy priesthood, to offer spiritual sacrifices acceptable to God through Jesus Christ" (1 Peter 2:5). The Christian service is not based on the theft of the ancient temple service, but is its transfiguration in the Holy Spirit. We might even say that the Church of Christ preserves symbolically, mystically, certain elements of Israel's worship service, which were made materially impossible by the destruction of the Temple — in particular, the sacrificial rites which the offering of Jesus' Passover actualizes in the Eucharist.

This must not be regarded as following the theories of substitution or rejection of the people of Israel. On the contrary, we see here the riches of Israel, to which the pagans are granted access in Christ, as Jesus showed in a prophetic gesture. In purifying the exterior court, the court of the pagans, in the Temple, he insisted that even the court of the Gentiles is pure, that the rules of ritual purity must be respected there, and henceforth that it too is holy. Even the court where the moneychangers and pigeon vendors stood (Matthew 21:12) is subject to the laws of holiness. Thus the pagans, too, have access to the holiness of Israel's Temple. Consequently, in the Christian liturgy, the pagans are granted access to Israel's service of God.

The Land

Finally, it can be said, still in the same line of thought and without presuming to take anything away from Israel, that there is a connection between the hope and the land, the earth. "Blessed are the meek, for they shall inherit the earth" (Matthew 5:5). The earth referred to is the land of Israel. Jesus' disciples have a right to the land, at least in the form of the hope for the Kingdom of God where all mankind will one day be gathered. The hope for this land does not cancel the promise made to Abraham.

By the way, the beatitude, "Blessed are the pure in heart, for they shall see God" (Matthew 5:8) can be explained within the context of the Temple, because it refers to a purity of heart that surpasses all legal purity. "They shall see God," because God is seen in the sanctuary; thus, they have access to the Temple. The hearts of those whom God purifies become like the Holy of Holies in the Temple, where Isaiah was able to see the glory of God.[6]

The Reign

In Christ, the pagans whom God calls have access to the history of Israel, to the Torah and the Bible, to Israel's prayer and festivals, to the land. They have access to the hope of the Kingdom of God. They learn, along with Israel, that they belong to no earthly "reign" or "kingdom." Israel knows this through historical experience, because it is one of the characteristics of the path by which God leads his people. God makes Israel aware that its vocation as a consecrated people dedicates it to God, to conform to his will, in the present world. And Israel is taught by God that no earthly reign can fulfill such a vocation. The Davidian kingdom was a disappointment, and Israel awaits the King-Messiah given by God. The Messiah will be the son of David, a king of justice and holiness. And Israel knows this. Israel is the only people who, historically, concretely, despite occasional arrangements, was in mortal

---

6. Cf. Isaiah 6:1-5. The Holy of Holies, or inner sanctuary, was situated at the back of the Temple. It was initially separated from the main hall by a door (cf. 1 Kings 6:31), which was replaced in the second Temple by a curtain (Matthew 27:51). The chief priest entered it only for the feasts of Yom Kippur and the Day of Atonement.

contradiction with the Roman Empire. This is why the Romans felt it necessary to exterminate Israel; and this is the reason for the exemplary, cruel, and merciless character of the two Jewish Wars.[7] Otherwise, given the weakness of the military forces in the provinces, the entire empire risked an explosion.

But the pagans who have access to the mystery of Christ have shaken off the bewitchment of Caesar, of Babel.[8] Man gives himself a fascinating image of his own power by deifying the state. Even though the state was born from the Christian experience in Europe and is the condition of political liberty, it can become an idol. It is even one of the strongest forms of idolatry that exists; it has become the most absolute substitute for God that men have been able to give themselves. We still see it in our days; and it is a tyrant god, feeding itself on its victims.

Israel is aware of this danger, and for this reason has been persecuted by tyrants over the centuries. The present problem is that Israel is also a state like others, and hence is experiencing a cruel apprenticeship in sovereignty.

But the people of Israel, the people of God, know well that every sovereign state can represent the most common and strongest idolatry, the absolute antithesis of God. This may explain why the confrontation between God and Caesar, as related in the Gospel, is so vigorous. The meaning is clear: "Render therefore to Caesar the things that are Caesar's, and to God the things that are God's" (Matthew 22:21). This does not mean sharing power. "Render to Caesar the things that are Caesar's" means that the coins belong to him; they bear his stamp, a sign of his ownership. But Jesus goes on to tell the Pharisees to "render

7. The first Jewish revolt against Rome (A.D. 66 to 70) was crushed first by Vespasian's campaigns in Galilee and Judea, followed by Titus's siege of Jerusalem in A.D. 70. Flavius Joseph, a privileged witness to this war, gives an account in *La Guerre des Juifs* (Paris: Editions de Minuit, 1977). The Second Jewish War, in Judea, took place under the Emperor Hadrian and repressed the uprising led by Bar Kokheba ("Son of the Star") in A.D. 132. He had presented himself as the Messiah and was recognized as such by some who saw him as "the star" that "shall come forth out of Jacob" (Numbers 24:17).

8. Cf. Genesis 11:1-9.

to God the things that are God's," that is, render to God the people which belong to him.

What have the pagans, now become Christians, made of these words? Is it still possible to have Christian empires? How can there still be hopes for the coming of the "reign" in this world, when Jesus says, "My kingship is not of this world" (John 18:36)? This revelation is one of the ways in which we are delivered from idolatry. Instead of being a cause for despair or sorrow, it is the cause of a far greater freedom, a far greater force. Herein lies the source of man's dignity, who knows that he is the son of God; and nothing in this world can reign over him, only God himself.

The Redemption

Finally, in Christ, the pagans participate in Israel's mission as servant and redeemer. Isaiah's four poems devoted to "the Servant" (Isaiah 42:1-9; 49:1-9; 50:4-9; 52:13; 53:12) simultaneously describe both an individual and Israel. This is what we have called the "corporate personality": the ambivalence, the oscillation between a person and a people. When commentaries — whether Christian or Jewish — say that the servant in question is Israel — the people — they are right. But the servant is also someone, a person, an individual servant. The two interpretations are not mutually exclusive. It is the same connection that exists between Jesus and his disciples, between the "Son of Man" and the people of the saints of the Most High. Rather than being opposed, the two meanings are mutually inclusive and interrelated.

The pagans participate in the vocation of Israel-the-Servant through Christ, who fulfills perfectly this vocation of servant, in a way that was previously unimaginable. They have the right, or rather the grace, to share the solitude and the faithfulness of Jesus-the-Servant of God, Son of God, and of Israel. They have the right and the grace to enter into the work of the redemption of sin, the work of redemption. In this way, the secret of the inexplicable suffering of the Elected People, in the figure of the Messiah, is revealed. It is Christ himself who is the cipher, the key which allows us to receive the unaccountable and unbearable suffering of Israel as a blessing.

This is what Jesus explains to the disciples on the road to Emmaus when he says to them: "O foolish men, and slow of heart to believe all that the prophets have spoken! Was it not necessary that the Christ should suffer these things and enter into his glory?" (Luke 24:25-26). Incomprehensible mystery for Israel, even when it hears these words. Mystery that is understandable only in the grace of the Messiah. It can be received only as a gift from on high. It is not a matter of intellectual assimilation. It is not a problem of incomprehension that must be further explained — and discussed. To understand it is a grace, the grace of Christ himself. And in this grace we receive the key to the secret of Israel's suffering, a key which remains incomprehensible to Israel itself, even when it glimpses and expresses the meaning of its suffering.

The pagans have the grace of entering into this work of redemption. They share the Messiah's mission. They are his brothers and sisters, the offspring of the brothers who share in the Beatitudes and through whom the world is judged and saved in the secret of human lives and history. They are those through whom evil is not only a source of blasphemy, a horror for sensible men, an attack on God, but becomes transformed into a source of blessing through forgiveness, as a pledge of redemption. But evil can take on this paradoxical aspect only to the extent that the disciples receive the understanding of the Scriptures and joyfully embrace this identification with the suffering Messiah who leads them to the heart of God and to all the riches of Israel.

We could continue this enumeration by reflecting on all the abundance of grace to which we have access "in Christ Jesus" (Romans 3:21 and following). He is the entryway, not only as the fulfillment of the gift made to Israel, but as the one who gives the pagans access to these same riches. "To the Jew first and also to the Greek" (Romans 1:16). It is the hidden mystery of Christ.

Repentance

This litany should lead us to a profound self-examination — if not personal then, at least, historical — concerning the conduct of pagan peoples who have embraced Christianity and who have received the Messiah's grace. "Christian" signifies precisely that: "one who has received the Messiah's grace." This is what was said at Antioch by those who were the first to designate Jesus' disciples as "Christians." If we wanted to bring the word up to date, we might designate them as "messianic," since "Christ," *Christos,* is the "anointed one," the "Messiah." "Christ" has become a proper name, but it refers to a mission: the proper name is "Jesus," Jesus, the Messiah.

Having thus entered into this grace and this vocation, we Christians should see how, historically, this grace has been, in a certain manner, inversed. Each of the elements of this litany should lead each of the pagan peoples to an outpouring of thanksgiving, in which they recognize God's gift to Israel and give thanks to God who has freely given them to share in it. It is the attitude of the one forgiven, of the prodigal son who says, "I am no longer worthy to be called your son" (Luke 15:19). And yet, his father refuses to heed him. This is the sign of an absolute, freely bestowed gift.

However, we can note that to each of these points in the litany there corresponds a sort of dark reversal, a diabolical, infernal perversion in which the persecution of Israel — of the Jews, to put it plainly — becomes the reverse sign, the blasphemous negation of the grace received. It is an exceedingly painful history and requires repentance.

Let us take an example which occurred frequently, and whose mechanism is known: the accusations of ritual crimes, which resulted in much bloodshed during the Middle Ages and modern times. These accusations emerged just when there was a homicidal tendency among Christian peoples. The accusation of ritual crimes, when the Jews were accused of killing Christian children so as to celebrate the Passover, led to massacres of the Jewish population. This is the mechanism where one accuses in order to attack. Rather than accepting as a gift what God gives them of the riches he has given to Israel, Christians have perversely rejected the Jews by completely denying their dignity in order to next exterminate them through persecution. The goal is characteristically annihilation.

The same can be said of the accusations that Jews have imperial designs on the world. For example, in both the Middle Ages and modern times, Jews have often been accused of wanting to possess the earth, to rule the world. And yet, strangely, at the same time, the ritual for the consecration of the kings of Judah was being used for the consecration of kings and emperors.[9] History is full of paradoxes of this type. And even though it has not been universally the case, the temptation remains permanent: the fate reserved for Jews is the test of whether the Christianized pagans have truly accepted Christ. It is really the absolute test. This is not simply a matter of the relationship between love of neighbor and love of God. The Jew remains, in a very precise sense, the sign of Election, and, hence, of Christ. To fail to recognize the Election of the Jews is to fail to recognize the Election of Christ. And it is to be unable to accept one's own election. The logic is implacable.

Let us take yet another example. The Letter to the Romans is completely centered on the fact that God's gifts are freely given, without any merit on our part. But this, in the confrontation between Israel and the nations, is often ignored. The reading of the Letter to the Romans has been disconnected from its internal logic. The final part, beginning with chapter 9, appears as a useless and irrelevant supple-

---

9. A precise indication can be found in the work of François Dupuigrenet-Desroussilles, *Dieu en son Royaume: La Bible dans la France d'autrefois, XIIIème-XVIIIème siècles*, Bibliothèque Nationale (Paris: Cerf, 1991), p. 18. "For Philippe de Mézières in the *Songe du vieil pèlerin*, the throne of France is the throne of David and the king a new Moses leading the people. The most curious effort of this type is the *Opus Davidicum* that the Italian Franciscan Giovanni Angelo Terzone de Lagonissa dedicated to Charles VIII of France. For him, the people of France descended from David and one day would return to Palestine. This astonishing work remained isolated, as the French kingdom could be Jewish only spiritually. Guillaume Michel, in his *Penser de royal mémoire*, which appeared in 1521 and employed rhetoric with virtuoso, makes an exaggerated use of the parallel between David and King Francis I."

ment. And the universality of sin pointed out at the beginning has not been interpreted as including pagans as well as Jews, and so is no longer understood as testifying to God's free gift to both, and to their freely given justification.

This led to the interpretations of the Middle Ages, the Reformation and Counter-Reformation, where the debate over the free gift of grace, or "grace versus works," took place outside of the historical context in which this was revealed with respect to Jews and pagans, whether Christians or not. Commentaries from these periods discuss the Law, works, and grace without once pronouncing the words *Jew* or *pagan*. Entire treatises on grace cite texts from the Letter to the Romans while completely ignoring its historical context and, hence, perverting its meaning. They have made the letter unintelligible.

For the pagan sinner it is a grace to have access in Christ to the riches of Israel. And for the Jew, who must also acknowledge that, regarding the Law, he too is a sinner, the coming of the pagan demonstrates the gratuitous and fecund nature of the gift he has received from God. God's free and unmerited gift becomes doubly apparent, mutually manifested by each to the other, through faith in Christ. Christ, in fully accomplishing the Law, opens, through grace, the riches of God's reign to all, both Jews and pagans. This is the theme of the Letter to the Romans. This is the mystery of God's plan.

The fact remains that many pagans and many Jews have not recognized Christ. But Jesus' disciples, if they are to be the "Catholic" Church, must be found among both Jews and pagans. By that very fact, the Church is Catholic "according to the whole," and is not linked to a particularity. Election according to a particularity is solely the Election of Israel. Catholic unity is the Assembly according to the whole of the Jews and the pagans.

Thus the Church of Christ must bear witness to the completely freely given and unearned nature of God's gifts, in an act of thanksgiving shared with Israel. In this world, the Church is called, through God's mercy, to be the pledge and the seed of the hope received of the "reign," already fulfilled in the Messiah of Israel, but not yet fully visible for either Jews or Gentiles.

What, then, is the significance of our position, disciples of Christ who share in Israel's hope while we proclaim its fulfillment? This is the specificity of the Christian mystery, which allows us to read, in the Scriptures and in the grace given both to Israel and to the pagans, the unfathomable depths of God's mystery. It can elude even those who are its beneficiaries. We must receive it as a grace, a source of humility, never as an exclusive privilege and still less as an excuse for our murderous iniquities.

This is the specific vocation of the Church of Jesus.

CHAPTER 11

Facing Israel — The Nations' Examination of Conscience

To conclude these days of prayer, let us share in Paul's thanksgiving pronounced in the Letter to the Ephesians (1:3-23). What he calls the mystery, the fact that Israel's election has been opened to the pagans, is for him a great blessing.

"Blessed be the God and Father of our Lord Jesus Christ, who has blessed us in Christ with every spiritual blessing in the heavenly places, even as he chose us in him before the foundation of the world, that we should be holy and blameless before him. He destined us in love to be his sons through Jesus Christ, according to the purpose of his will, to the praise of his glorious grace, which he freely bestowed on us in the Beloved. In him we have redemption through his blood, the forgiveness of our trespasses, according to the riches of his grace, which he lavished upon us. For he has made known to us in all wisdom and insight the mystery of his will, according to his purpose, which he set forth in Christ as a plan for the fullness of time, to unite all things in him (to sum up all things in the Messiah), things in heaven and things on earth. In him, according to the purpose of him who accomplishes all things according to the counsel of his will, we who first hoped in Christ (Paul is referring to the Jews) have been destined and appointed to live for the praise of his glory. In him you also (the pagans), who have heard the word of truth, the gospel of your salvation, and have believed in him, were sealed with the promised Holy Spirit, which is the guarantee of our inheritance until we acquire possession of it, to the praise of his glory. For this reason, because I have heard of your faith in the Lord Jesus and your love toward all the saints (he is referring to the Church of Jerusalem), I do not cease to give thanks for you, remembering you in my prayers, that the God of our Lord Jesus Christ, the Father of glory, may give you a spirit of wisdom and of revelation in the knowledge of him, having the eyes of your hearts enlightened, that you may know what is the hope to which he has called you, what are the riches of his glorious inheritance in the saints, and what is the immeasurable greatness of his power in us who believe, according to the working of his great might, which he accomplished in Christ when he raised him from the dead and made him sit at his right hand in the heavenly places, far above all rule and authority and power and dominion, and above every name that is named, not only in this age but also in that which is to come; and he has put all things under his feet and has made him the head over all things for the church, which is his body, the fullness of him who fills all in all."

On Christian Anti-Semitism

The time has now come to take up the question of Christian attitudes toward Israel. Until now, I have posed the question only from within the perspective of the Christian faith — not with respect to a Jewish interlocutor — meditating on the grace the Church has received from God and reflecting on how the Church has both sinned and been faithful to God. Up to now, I have spoken of the mystery of Israel as a fundamental question for Christianity.

Now I should like to speak to you in supposing that a non-Christian Jew were among us.

First of all, we need to recognize God's gift to Israel, since it is an essential part of our faith. No one can be a Christian, a disciple of Christ, without recognizing that this gift of God is irrevocable. Unless we recognize this, we cannot claim to share in Israel's gift. To recognize the gift of God is to, like Saint Paul, give thanks for Israel, and give thanks for the history of the world's salvation.

In addition, today, we must accept that Israel be itself, that Jews be themselves and define themselves according to their own understanding. We must not idealize. Like Christians, the Jews are a people of sinners who must convert themselves, who are called to be faithful to the grace they have received. Today, a limited number of persons in the Church are discovering the riches of the Talmudic tradition.[1] It should be pointed out, however, that Judaism cannot be summed up by rabbinism. There are internal crises in the Jewish world, often related to those of Western rationality. Let us accept — and this is part of the act of faith — our neighbor as he is, as the person God has permitted him to be. We must accept him in all his diversity, which is sometimes disconcerting, with all his human weaknesses, limitations, and sins.

Finally, Christian anti-Semitism is not just another example of racism. It is truly a sin — one whose enormity implies a profound infidelity to Christ's grace. What Christians attack in Israel is a reflection of what they reject in Christ. It is a rejection they do not admit as such. For the Christian conscience, what is called the "Jewish question" is not merely the problem of a racial, ethnic, or cultural minority.[2] In every people, whenever there is a foreign population, we see xenophobic reactions. These are found in all peoples, cultures, or tribes — whether archaic or extremely developed. On the other hand, when this mechanism is triggered in Christians in regard to Jews, it immediately touches their faith. The Jews are who they are only because they are, first of all, witnesses to the Election. Christians who reject them, whether deliberately or not, are engaging in an abusive or blasphemous appropriation of the Election. It is a concrete refusal of the real-

1. The Talmud is the study of the Torah. It is composed of two elements: the *Michna*, the first written summary of the oral law composed from 30 B.C. to A.D. 220, and the *Guemara* (called 'Talmud' in the restricted sense of the word), an explanation of and commentary on the *Michna*, which was completed in the sixth century. See *Le Talmud*, vol. 1, *Guide et lexiques* (Paris: F.S.J.U.-Ramsay, 1995).

2. The expression "Jewish question" comes from Karl Marx. Cf. Jean-Paul Sartre, *Réflexions sur la question juive* (Paris: Gallimard, Folio-Essais, 1954).

ity of God's gift, of God's ways. Those who have a good background in history can reflect on the different aspects these rejections have taken during the various epochs of the Church's existence. These sins have often left their brand on a civilization, a people.

But God has always inspired saints within his Church, people in whom the Holy Spirit dwells, so that the body of Christ can be purified. It may be a grace of our times, after two thousand years of unhealed wounds in Christ's body, that this awareness arises now, at the moment when the sins of the Church are becoming evident to the Church herself. I detect a certain spiritual logic in the fact that anti-Judaism is now emerging as a problem internal to Christianity just when ecumenism is being revealed as a mission, a grace, for the Church. The two are not unrelated, since both entail great soul searching as to the degree of faithfulness or infidelity of the Western peoples to the grace given to them close to two thousand years ago. Facing her current dispossession, the Western Church is beginning to notice that she does not hold the monopoly on Christianity, that she is not the Kingdom of God on earth, even if she might have thought so at certain periods in history. She notices that Christianity does not belong to anyone except God himself, and is given only to those whom God calls.

Christian anti-Semitism is still alive. This hatred reveals something of Christ's Passion, of the scene in which he is insulted, ridiculed. The image of Christ, thus reversed, becomes unbearable. Christ is unrecognizable when those who carry his name give a distorted image of him, when he is disfigured by the very ones who claim to belong to him. If Christ was "made to be sin" for us (2 Corinthians 5:21), his image has been disfigured by this sin, the sin of his disciples.

The matter in question is of enormous import, regardless of the causes and of the contribution made by each historical period. Until the third century, there was a conflict within the Church, a polemic to which the New Testament bears witness. The Christians were most probably defending themselves against the synagogue, and hostility was undoubtedly mutual. The historians can tell this better than I can. But even after seventeen centuries, the traces of this hostility remain unbearably present. God's infinite mercy is needed for the face of

Christ to appear in all its truth, since the face, the image of Christ, is that shown by Christians.

The Economy of Grace

There remains the problem of the acceptance or refusal of Christ by Israel and its leaders, which is real, and cannot be denied. This drama is at the center of Saint Matthew's Gospel, even to such absolutely terrible phrases as that in the apocalyptic discourse in the Temple: "There will not be left here one stone upon another, that will not be thrown down" (Matthew 24:1). This is the judgment before which the figure of the Messiah places all men, including Israel. It is found in Scripture and is a part of the Christian faith.

But it is very different for Christians to hear these words in a way corresponding with the Spirit of God. We cannot forget what has been done with these words: they have been turned into murderous, homicidal accusations. By their use of these words, Christians have committed blasphemy against Christ. We must remember this lack of understanding. We must neither be unfaithful to the mysteries of Scripture nor deny them, even if our failure to understand makes them difficult to bear. These words must not be transformed into a blasphemous judgment of others, because God does not charge us with judging others.

Is our reading of the New Testament truly Christian? Our commentaries too often testify against us, against Christian faithfulness to God. It is the entire economy of grace that is thus overturned. It is not just a specific injustice; it is the entire faithfulness to the gift of God that has become obscured. This obscuring of our vision, this blindness to God's gift leads to a still greater infidelity. It is well known that the logic of sin is to provoke callousness, hardness of heart; that is, the failure to recognize our own reality. The sinner does not know that he sins, and is unaware that he cannot escape his sin on his own. He can only be delivered from this sinful state if God gives him his grace and reverses the infernal process. Callousness is found at the heart of the Gospel, as at the heart of Scripture. This callousness is the self-inflicted blindness of the sinner; he is all the more miserable for not seeing the extent of his misery, and not even being aware of it. What, then, is our situation with respect to the mystery of Israel?

There is so much in Scripture that we are far from having explored, or re-explored, because of the extent to which spiritually grave and costly prejudices have hidden much that is nonetheless clearly stated. The reexamination of these words presupposes an immense effort, and perhaps some risky hypotheses. But the spiritual stakes are of the greatest importance for the Church's faith. Through such a reexamination, the Church can rediscover the specific grace and vision of herself that she can and must receive and convey.

It has to be said also that there has been little positive acknowledgment from the Jewish side of the existence of Christianity. And often the recognition has been limited to accusations of blasphemy and persecution. Such a situation is to be regretted, but we must ask ourselves if it is due only to unwillingness or refusal.

It could be argued that the Christian welcome of Jews and Judaism as a blessing could bring about a greater recognition by Jews of Christians and Christianity. Only time will tell, and only God knows the outcome. But nothing can be hoped for in this regard as long as the liability of centuries of Christian persecution of Jews has not been overcome.

The Church's Vocation

The Jewish people remains what it is, with the promises and the demands of its faithfulness, of its survival, of its existence. The pagans remain, nations who have not yet been touched by the Gospel, like the "non-evangelized zones" that could be seen on missionary maps at the beginning of the century. But the expansion of Christianity is not to be compared with the hoisting of the French flag in the Sahara. The Cross is not erected in a territory; it is inscribed in contrite hearts. The Cross implies a conversion, and conversion is always an unfinished process, contrary to what the world's empires may think. Paganism remains a perpetual temptation for every human being, until he goes to God. This is true of individuals as it is true of peoples and civilizations. Any people, simply because it remains a people of sinners, reverts to idolatry and to some extent ceases to be Christian. Baptism is received once and for all by the grace of Christ, but sin remains and gives the lie to this grace. Our unfaithfulness is opposed to God's faithfulness. We can remain Christian only through God's generosity; and we must constantly give thanks for his faithfulness. Our identity as Christians is entirely a gift from God; it is never a possession to be appropriated by man.

What, then, is the Church's vocation in this world where, confronted with Christ and its own destiny, Israel continues on its way with an unsatisfied hope, and where the pagans remain, often unaware that they await redemption? They may not be aware of the waiting, but God is: God awaits the redemption of the pagan nations. The pagans do not necessarily desire redemption and resurrection. Can we assume that there is a desire for the true God in the pagans' heart? This is not always the case.

Whatever the case, if the Church is faithful to her vocation, she will present to Israel's eyes a recognizable figure of the Messiah. How will Israel be able to recognize some of the Messiah's traits in the Church? At what cost? How much love for the unique and true God must be shown by Christians? How much forgiveness? How much recognition of God's blessing and faithfulness? How much consciousness of the meaning of redemption? How can Israel, drawn to God and chosen by God, recognize the face of its own Messiah in the Church? How can Israel recognize the pagan-Christians as a gift of grace that God has bestowed on it, an increase given to Israel by God? Obviously, the minimum condition would be that the Christian cease to appear as a vital threat, someone who wants to divest Israel of its own identity, to kill or persecute it, and instead becomes, for Israel, a sign of the superabundant blessing of God.

Of course, Israel has a part to play in all this. But let us remember the Lord's teaching: "Why do you see the speck that is in your brother's eye, but do not notice the log that is in your own eye?" (Matthew 7:3-5).

It is not our place to judge anybody's faithfulness. Let the Church account for what she has done with the grace she has received!

The Promise

At this point, I must share with you a prayer that is so audacious that I hardly dare express it out loud.

Do you remember what I said at the beginning of these talks about the first Church, the mother-Church, the Church of Jerusalem? The account of its disappearance is a cruel and enlightening page in the Church's history. In order to remain "Catholic" in the original sense — that is, "according to the whole" — recognizes, in a single gift of God's grace, both the *Ecclesia ex circumcisione* (the Church born from circumcision) and the *Ecclesia ex gentibus* (the Church born from the pagan nations). Thus, the Church is the Church "of the Jews" and "of the pagans"; both were called "Christians" by the people of Antioch.

James, the "brother" — the term actually means the "cousin" — of the Lord, is the first "bishop" of this Jerusalem Church, which was composed solely of Jews who were disciples of Jesus.[3] There is no point in reminding you of the opening chapters of the Acts of the Apostles. Paul was subsequently to mobilize the generosity of all the new churches, made up of either both Jews and pagans or a majority of pagans, to come to the aid of this Church in Jerusalem, which was eliminated over the course of history, first by Byzantium and then by Islam.

This is a tragedy whose consequences are still felt by the Eastern Churches. Especially after the Council of Chalcedon, Byzantium imposed its language, Greek, and its liturgy on the Christian communities of countries where the Semitic tradition had been prevalent.[4]

3. Cf. Galatians 1:19.

4. Convoked by the Emperor Marcian, a council was held at Chalcedon in 451. On March 21, 453, Pope Leo approved the decisions concerning faith in Christ, but did not recognize the privileges granted to Byzantium. Through this council, Byzantium's appropriation of the Eastern Church became apparent. The Church of Alexandria and the Syriac Church became largely separated from Rome. Scripture attests to the link

Whether Catholic or not, the communities of the patriarchy of Antioch and Alexandria survived only at the price of their resistance and, often, their isolation. The Chaldean tradition has retained Aramaic as their liturgical language. But all that has little to do with the current reality of the Jewish people.

Contemporary history has placed before us another paradoxical event: the rebirth of the State of Israel. This State was politically inspired by the secularized West and its culture. Even if this is still the object of vigorous internal debates, Israel introduced the idea of a secular state granting equal rights to all its citizens, regardless of their religion, into the Middle East. The paradox is that the people of Israel, while claiming its specificity as such, intends to make its entry among other nations on the Western model, which is becoming universal. In this situation, a "Church," an *Ecclesia ex circumcisione*, as it is designated in a mosaic at Saint Sabina in Rome, once again becomes conceivable.

You know this better than anybody, since Dom Grammont recently decided to reopen the venerable monastery of Abu-Gosh in Israel.[5] He sent three monks there, among them Brother Jean-Baptiste.

---

between these churches and the Church of Jerusalem (cf. Acts of the Apostles 2:10; 6:9; 18:24-28 for Alexandria; cf. Acts of the Apostles 11:19-26, and Galatians 2:11 for Antioch). The presence of an important Jewish community in Alexandria, as well as in Edessa (north of Antioch, in non-Hellenized Syria), no doubt explains the rapid spread of Christianity. The hellenization of these Christian communities began in the third century. The councils of Ephesus (431) and Chalcedon engendered profound separations and tragically weakened these Eastern Churches. In February 1988, a common christological expression was approved by the Catholic and Orthodox Copt Churches. In June 1984, a christological and pastoral declaration was signed between the Catholic Church and the Orthodox Syrian Church. The dogmatic reconciliation between the Catholic Church and the Assyrian Church of the East took place on November 11, 1994 through a common christological declaration.

5. Dom Paul Grammont was born on February 20, 1911, in Troyes and made his monastic profession at Mesnil Saint-Loup (Aube) on September 19, 1929. He was elected prior in 1939 and founded a study house in Cormeilles-en-Parisis with the religious community of Sainte Françoise Romaine. After the Second World War, the monks and nuns joined to give new life to the Bec-Hellouin Abbey, which had been deconsecrated after the French Revolution. Dom Paul became the abbot in 1948. In 1976, brothers and

You sustain them by your prayer, in the hope that you will be able to establish a new monastic community alongside theirs in the near future.[6]

This *Ecclesia ex circumcisione* which evangelized the *Ecclesia ex gentibus* was awakened from its long sleep by an initial gesture from Pope Pius XII. In 1954, Cardinal Tisserand, head of the Congregation for the Eastern Churches, had encouraged the creation of an association dedicated to such an awakening, the "Oeuvre Saint-Jacques l'Apôtre," under the aegis of the Latin patriarch of Jerusalem, Archbishop Albert Gori. The first mass *ad experimentum* said in Hebrew, according to the Syriac rite, was celebrated in Haifa in 1956. Finally, in 1957 — well before the liturgical reform of Vatican II — Pope Pius XII granted Cardinal Tisserand the usage of Hebrew in the Latin rite for what we today call the "Liturgy of the Word," and for the end of the Mass, starting with the "Lord's Prayer."

I began to discover all this thanks to Father Jean-Roger Henné, an Assumptionist who dedicated his life to this Hebrew-speaking community. I met Father Henné in 1951 when, still a seminarian, I made my first pilgrimage to the Holy Land.[7] He made me promise that, once or-

---

sisters from Bec-Hellouin respectively installed themselves in Israel, at the Monastery of Abu Gosh, and reestablished monastic life at Mesnil Saint-Loup. Having reached the age of 75, Dom Grammont retired from the abbey's direction in 1986. He died on July 30, 1989, and is buried in the choir of the Bec-Hellouin Abbey. Crusaders settled in the village of Abu Gosh in the eleventh century and renamed it Emmaus. They built a church (Saint Mary of the Resurrection) in memory of the encounter of the Resurrected Jesus with the pilgrims on the road to Emmaus (cf. Luke 24). The territory of Abu Gosh became the property of France in 1873. In 1899, Benedictines from La Pierre-qui-Vire came to pray there, but did not stay. In 1976, three Benedictine monks belonging to the Congrégation des Olivétains at Bec-Hellouin arrived.

6. The monks eventually built their monastery as an abbey, and the sisters of Sainte Françoise Romaine subsequently came to join them. Father Jean-Baptiste Gourion became its first abbot in 1999. The Patriarch of Jerusalem charged him with overseeing the Hebrew-speaking Catholic communities in Israel, and on November 9, 2003, he was ordained as their bishop. He died on June 23, 2005, and was succeeded by Father Pierbattista Pizzaballa, O.F.M., as the pastor of this "small flock," with episcopal powers granted by the Pope.

7. Father Henné died on September 5, 1979.

dained, I would join him in serving this small, very small flock. Until now, I have not been able to keep my word.

Almost every year between 1951 and the time I was appointed a parish priest, I made the pilgrimage to the holy sites, accompanied by university students. I followed the growth and trials of that impoverished community — fragile and wounded. Its members — regardless of their origins — are presently subjected to every contradiction: those that the Jewish people have always had to bear; those that, over the centuries, Christians have endured in that so complex country. Among the community are a majority of consecrated individuals — priests, nuns, and lay people. Everything seems to suggest that God wanted to bring together in this strange little flock only those called to bear the highest witness to charity and perseverance, individuals dedicated to holiness. And yet, what weaknesses, what poverty, what wounds, what tensions . . .

I was given the grace, about a year and a half ago, to be able to visit your brothers from Bec-Hellouin in their Abu Gosh foundation. The three of them were a sign of peace in a suffering and divided Hebrew-speaking community, which was rejected by most of the local congregations. While praying and sharing with your brothers the impressions gathered from my month's stay in the Holy Land, I came to feel that they were a promise for the future of this Church *ex circumcisione*. What will that future be? Only God knows. Perhaps, after all, this Hebrew-speaking community, in its hidden and humiliated condition, gives Christians of Gentile origin the sign of the Suffering Servant and the Lamb.

And yet, if the Church granted it an existence in its own specificity, this group could fulfill, in association with the Arab-Christian communities, the mission entrusted by Jesus to his disciples. Between Judaism and Islam, between the Arab and Western cultures, among all the contradictory political claims being made in that region, who else could be called on to live this Beatitude: "Blessed are the peacemakers, for they shall be called sons of God"?[8] Saint Paul says of Christ, Son of

8. Cf. Matthew 5:9.

God: "In his blood is our peace . . ."; he has made us both one, and has "broken down the dividing wall of hostility."[9] It is this witness that the torn and divided Middle East awaits from Christians.

During this trip I came to feel that the way in which the Hebrew-speaking community was viewed both by Jewish Israelis and established Christian groups was beginning to change. I entrust it to your prayer. Because if God permits it to regain its identity within the Church, it will be an inestimable blessing for the faith of all. It would be the sign and pledge of God's faithfulness to his Promise. It would root the Christians' mission more deeply in the history of salvation, as the Council of Vatican II so vigorously reminds us.

Marana Tha

Christian hope is thus marked by anticipation. Through God's gifts we anticipate the fulfillment of all things; and yet God is not yet everything for everyone.

The temptation for Christians is to imagine that the reign of God has already arrived. This attitude is what we observe when churches substitute themselves for the reign of God; they convey nothing more than the image of a human society that uses God as a tool. Christian hope, on the contrary, is the experience of the Holy Spirit and of the resurrection by men and women still inhabited by death. They still exist in the flesh and yet they are already living in the Spirit. They share in the life of the Resurrected Christ while knowing that they will still have to pass through death, and they share in the communion of the Holy Spirit while they are still divided.

Almost systematically, we forget that Christians share the hope of Israel brought to its climax in the figure of the crucified Messiah. But while Israel might be nostalgic for what has been promised to it — a sign in this world, a land, a people, a recognized social existence — the brutal paradox of two thousand years of Christian history is that West-

9. Cf. Ephesians 2:13-17.

ern nations have claimed this hope and these promises for themselves and have attempted to realize them through their own means. The temptation is always to imagine the Kingdom of God as the visible and immediate fulfillment of justice through human power. But man can live in justice only if he acknowledges that he himself is unjust. Otherwise, man substitutes human injustice for divine justice. He reverts to paganism, and becomes Godless and hopeless, and forgets Israel's prophecy.

Through faith in the crucified Messiah, Christian nations have been indebted to the divine hope expressed by Israel. And yet they have relegated the very people chosen by God to bear witness to this hope to the margins of their societies, abandoned to poverty and rejection, dispossessed of their property, their roots, and their identity. Was it not the Jewish people who were for fifteen centuries in Europe the most visible witness to eschatology? They were a people of witnesses in spite of themselves, living in faithfulness to God to the point of martyrdom, in sin perhaps, but they were nonetheless witnesses that the Kingdom of God is not of this world. Do the martyrdom and messianic expectation of the Jews have no meaning, no price, for the Church which awaits the return of her Savior, which awaits the Parousia of the Savior of all?

1995-2002

Talks given in Tel Aviv, Paris,
Brussels, and Washington, D.C.

CHAPTER 12

Israel and the Gentiles

I accepted the invitation for this conference at the University of Tel Aviv with great emotion. It allows me to be in the land of Israel on the "Day of the Shoah," tomorrow, and to take part in the ceremony to be held at Yad Vashem, commemorating the fiftieth anniversary of the liberation of the concentration camps.

I have not visited the Yad Vashem Memorial since the summer of 1973, when I decided to spend a day there in fasting, meditation, and prayer.

I had found a relatively secluded place to sit. After several hours, the guardian, obviously concerned, came to me and said, "Don't grieve, say a *Kaddish* and go back home." And he handed me the text. And I did what he had told me to do, giving silent thanks to God for this guardian who had comforted me, just as the angel comforted Elijah in the wilderness (1 Kings 19:1-8).

I reveal this experience publicly today to explain the spirit in which I speak to you.

I should like to share with you a few thoughts on the destiny of

---

Talk given at the University of Tel Aviv on April 26, 1995 and published in the French edition of the *Osservatore romano* on May 2, 1995. Translated by Rebecca Howell Balinski.

"All Israel," that is, all of the Jewish people, those in the Diaspora as well as those assembled in the State of Israel.

I shall be able to explore only a few of the innumerable riches contained in the words spoken to Abraham: "By your descendants shall all the nations of the earth bless themselves" (Genesis 22:18).

The Loss of All the Nations

But, first of all, on this 50th anniversary, we are again asking ourselves why, just over half a century ago, God did not act as he had in times past, when he removed Lot and his family from Sodom and Gomorrah before the brimstone and fire rained down on these cities (Genesis 19:1-29).

Did God forget his promise? Did he repudiate his words transmitted by Hosea (11:8-9): "How can I give you up, O Ephraim! How can I hand you over, O Israel! How can I make you like Admah! How can I treat you like Zeboiim! My heart recoils within me, my compassion grows warm and tender. I will not execute my fierce anger, I will not again destroy Ephraim; for I am God and not man, the Holy One in your midst, and I will not come to destroy."

These are terrible questions on which we Christians and Jews, believers and nonbelievers, have been reflecting since the opening of this conference.

It is in our century that an unprecedented historical horror has occurred. In the plan to annihilate the Jewish people, men of all nations were implicated and, thus, responsible — directly or indirectly, as initiators or accomplices, through cynicism or through silence. This, at least, is what we have discovered by examining events after half a century. And the only divine response to this plan for annihilation would have been the destruction of all humanity, a new flood.

But God swore to Noah: "I will never again . . . destroy every living creature as I have done" (Genesis 8:21). This Noahic covenant with all of humanity leaves the field open for the freedom of men, capable of both the best and the worst. God has left in man's hands the power to annihilate humanity, a power that the conference on atomic weapons presently taking place in New York is trying to limit.

Therefore, to answer our question, "Why did God remain silent?" the Torah would urge us to ask: Why did God remain faithful to the covenant made with Noah, even when it meant that his people had to pay an unbearable price?

I do not believe that we have any answer other than this: together we Jews find ourselves survivors of the Shoah, we are alive. Together, all nations, despite humanity's suicidal power, of which Hiroshima was a symptom, find themselves alive. Together, to confront the unanswerable question regarding our future, we must reexamine the promise made to Abraham: "By your descendants shall all the nations of the earth bless themselves" (Genesis 22:18).

Because it is clear that the question regarding the future of the Jewish people cannot be raised without simultaneously questioning the destiny of all nations in the world.

The Jewish people cannot live "in a separate room" or withdraw from humanity. They would destroy themselves. This destruction is precisely what Hitler wished to accomplish and to which the kings of the earth would consent (Psalm 2:2). And reciprocally, the Gentiles know that to wish to destroy the earth would lead humanity to suicide.

The Salvation of All Nations

Regarding the benediction given to Abraham and the link it establishes between his descendants and the nations of the earth, there is a lesson to be learned from the past two thousand years of our history.[1]

If there is one thing that belongs specifically to the Jewish people, it is the Bible. And yet, for two thousand years, transmitted by Christian predication and translated into all languages, it has come to be venerated as the Word of God by a multitude of nations. All mankind

---

1. Cf. J.-M. Lustiger, "Let My People Go," talk given at Yale University on November 2, 1992, in *NRT* 115 (1993), pp. 481-495.

knows or discovers it; all mankind can receive it as a divine word that is destined for them as well as the Jews.

Men and women throughout the world receive from the Bible the consciousness of belonging to a unique history, the history of humanity. In contrast to all mythologies, the biblical account of creation reveals the mystery of God and allows men to discover their dignity and destiny through the history of the people of Israel who bear witness to God.

And it should be noted that contemporary forms of universality — scientific rationality and technology, human rights (albeit still far from being widely observed), the often denied but nevertheless generally acclaimed human solidarity for the good of each individual and of all — could never have been born or been imposed with such force if they had not been nourished by the biblical revelation.

This historical observation raises two questions:

- How can and should Jews consider the nations that receive and make their own the Revelation first made to Israel?
- How can and should the nations (or Gentiles) consider the Jews from whom they have received this Word?

In the past, there existed within Christianity a determination to dispossess, indeed to exterminate, the legitimate depository of this Revelation so as to appropriate this treasure. Are the non-Jews who today believe in the Word of God also usurpers? Can they claim to receive this Word without asking to become Jews? Can they still be considered ignorant worshipers of idols?

Through the texts of the Bible received in faith, the Gentiles, including those nations where no Jews reside, have a representation of the Jewish people. These believers cannot help but identify in some way with this people and its history. One of the most striking examples of this identification is that of the black Africans deported to the New World as slaves.

What view do these Gentiles have of the Jewish people, not only of their past, but of their present and future?

The Destiny of Israel — Singular and Universal

Regarding sin and death, as well as deliverance and life, the respective fates of Jews and Gentiles are indissolubly linked. Because of its Election and the Law, Israel, bearer of the messianic promise, "shall stand as an ensign to the peoples" (Isaiah 11:10). But precisely because of this promise of messianic salvation, the nations are called by God to enter into his Covenant with Israel and to "gather as the people of the God of Abraham" (cf. Psalm 47:9; Ezra 6:21; Isaiah 2:2-4; 66:18-22).

To the traditional query, "Will it be good for the Jews?" we might add, "Is it good for humanity?" The two questions are inseparable.

Only the biblical revelation formulates the relationship of the singular to the universal in these terms. Because, if the Jewish people are not a people "like others," it is, first of all, because they were created as people of God. It is that Election that constitutes their uniqueness.

God, who chose Israel to reveal himself, is God of the universe, the One whom all nations will recognize. The Creator of all men chose one people so as to make them the "instrument" — "a polished arrow, in his quiver" (Isaiah 49:2), his servant "set apart" — for fulfilling his plan of universal salvation.

Thus, the particular history of this people has been arranged for the salvation of all peoples. But this people's history has evolved not according to the ambition of empires and nations who seek to dominate all others. It is God alone, the unique God, who reigns over all peoples, and through him all peoples discover their equal dignity.

We all know what terrible directions paganized messianism can take. This messianism, deprived of the unction of the Holy Spirit, is reduced to a political, social, or ethnic imperialism.

Here, then, we come face-to-face with the paradox of the destiny of "All Israel."

The children of Israel have now been gathered together in a state like others — neither more nor less — and that is legitimate and necessary. The State was founded by the descendants of the people that God has called to be a people "not like others," but "for others," because of his plan for universal salvation.

And what is true for this nation of Jews living in the recently created State of Israel is also true for members of the Jewish people dispersed among the nations of which they are citizens. Yet their vocation of bearing witness depends not on human power but on God.

The destiny of "All Israel" is to be constantly surpassed by its destiny.

CHAPTER 13

From Jules Isaac to John Paul II: Questions for the Future

The signatories of Seligsberg had been optimistic. Jules Isaac had knocked at the door. The Second Vatican Council had opened it with the Declaration *Nostra Aetate*. From that moment on, we were to move along the path of mutual recognition of Jews and Christians. But it proved to be impossible to bypass a bloody two-millennia-old list of grievances. To plan our paths for the future, it was essential to clarify and come to terms with the past.

Despite misunderstandings and objections, Pope John Paul II undertook this task with boldness, love, and respect. He was prepared for it. He was acquainted with the Jewish condition. Jews were his neighbors, his fellow students, and his friends. Their customs as well as their memories of persecution were familiar to him. He had seen their annihilation in his suffering homeland. After the war, it was in the ancient culture of Central Europe, to which so many Jewish intellectuals and artists have contributed, that he showed his knowledge of the world and of history. He is the first Pope to have known by direct experience,

Talk at the European Jewish Congress, Paris, January 28-29, 2002. Translated by Msgr. Richard Malone for the *Osservatore romano*, English edition, March 2002.

something that is no longer possible, the world of the Jewish communities of Central Europe.

After Auschwitz

At the time when Karol Wojtyla began his pontificate, the generation of the contemporaries of the Shoah, at least the Europeans, had begun to emerge from their silence. Then "those who did not know" detected the sentiment of nihilism that marks this generation, the rejection of belief and hope, the annihilation of memory. Henceforth, Auschwitz has come to stand for the symbol of a memory burned to ashes. Auschwitz has reduced to nothing all that preceded it, the ancient Europe. Between Jews and Christians, for twenty years now, certain events publicized by the media, as soon as they happened, revived polemics, nurtured suspicions, and reopened old wounds: those of the Shoah and of the centuries when Jews were regularly persecuted in Christian Europe. Who would not feel bitterness that these fragile relations are constantly in danger of being broken off? However, in these circumstances, there have been enough men and women of good heart and lovers of the truth to pacify these recurring conflicts, to dispel misunderstandings and restore confidence.

Renewed Vision

John Paul II, for his part, has taken initiatives that have had an incredible symbolic impact. He could only do this thanks to the determination and courage of Jewish leaders.

I will not insist on the diplomatic agreement established between the State of Israel and the Vatican. The text is surprising, because of its religious and historical content.

I wish to mention here two symbolic deeds, among many others, which have led world opinion to perceive the strength of the Church's commitment in this area. When the Pope visited the great synagogue of Rome, his photograph with the chief Rabbi did more than any lengthy speech.

His pilgrimage to the Holy Land, his visit to Israel, his prayer at the Wailing Wall, all but overwhelmed the most hostile, indifferent, or skeptical minds.

At the same time, Pope John Paul II has developed a wide-ranging teaching on the relationship of Christians with the Jewish people. The Pope asks Christians to discover the Jewish people by looking at them, not just in the Bible, but also in the history of the last two millennia. I hope that the many addresses given over the years by the highest authority of the Christian world will be gathered into a book. They call philosophers and theologians, historians and sociologists, as well as politicians, to a new undertaking. For this reflection understands human history in the light of Revelation. It invites us to understand the meaning, for all people, of the Election of the Jewish people. Misunderstanding or renouncing this Election would deprive the history of salvation that founds the Christian faith — and perhaps all human history as well — of all its meaning.

The Service of Humanity

An enormous task has been accomplished in Christian and Jewish minds: the clarification and recognition of the responsibility of Christians in the tragedy of the Second World War; tying together the broken threads of a two thousand-year-old common history, of a common culture; to tell one another of the accumulated grievances even in their harsh truth, so that there is nothing unspoken among those who have inherited this history.

The task we face now is to reestablish the continuity of European history beyond the nihilism of the Shoah, to rediscover a dialogue that was started, broken-off, and then resumed, over two millennia. Thus, together we will discover that Auschwitz did not put an end to history since, accepting the whole past, we have the common will to live our common future for the service of humanity.

Who will speak of the spiritual greatness of those who were its architects, of the faith and generosity that they showed? Who will tell of the divine inspiration that guided them? Who will speak of the prayer of so many men and women who laid this plan before God? Little by little we intuit that, in those times of misfortune and hatred, the righteous have written a history composed of kindness, respect, humanity, and holiness, expressing the power of the biblical Word.

Toward Genuine Dialogue

We have reached an historic moment when a true dialogue, broken off almost two thousand years ago, can begin again; a dialogue, it is true, carried on in low voices by eminent souls too soon forgotten. It will not, of course, do away with the opposition or differences between Jews and Christians. A deeper reciprocal understanding of the Word of God will bring us to understand with respect what the Spirit gives to each to understand and to believe. Christians and Jews will find they are necessary for each other in a more intense and stronger vision of the greatness of the gift of God and of the beauty of human destiny.

The dialogue between John Paul II and Emmanuel Levinas[1] is an example of this. Biblical Revelation, as the Jewish tradition received it, and as the Church, through her faith in Christ, accepts it, is an inexhaustible treasure for the future of humanity.

---

1. Emmanuel Levinas (1905-1995) was a Jewish French philosopher born in Lithuania. Banking on both Judaism and the thinking of Husserl and Heidegger, he strove to root ethics anew in the experience of "the other" (instead of the self).

CHAPTER 14

What Can Jews and Christians Hope for When They Meet?

C an a keen observer consider that most problems have been solved
between the Jewish people and the Catholic Church since dramatic gestures were made on both sides, especially by Pope John
Paul II and Israeli officials?

The truth is that these events allow the work of discernment only
to begin. Such a task will appear as a more and more pressing priority
to any person aware that this is a vital question for both Catholics and
Jews in their mutual relationship.

Before all, however, they still have to get to know each other
better. The first point I want to make is that this should prove more
fruitful than expected. But for the time being, we first have to acknowledge that such an undertaking remains unaccomplished by Christians
as well as by Jews, and this will be dealt with in a second part.

Address to the World Jewish Congress, Brussels, April 22-23, 2002. Translated by Jean
Duchesne.

Getting to Know Each Other

To start with, how does the average church-going Christian believer usually picture the Jewish people, or the Jews?

How Christians Read the Bible

His main — and decisive — source of information is the Bible. The dynamic identity of the Jewish people, whose sacred history emerges from the biblical text, is the practical structure of Western civilization. The world of the Bible, which a Jew is entitled to consider as his own heritage, has also become the womb of all the visions of history and society that can be found in every culture inspired by the Christian faith.

The New Testament was written by Jews, and remains incomprehensible without sufficient knowledge of Jewish life and hopes both in the Holy Land and in the Diaspora. Everyone knows how the documents may have been interpreted in contradictory, harmful ways, even within the Church. But there is no need here to recall the details of all that the latest popes, from John to Paul to John Paul, have achieved in order to reject the charge of "deicide" and the teaching of contempt.

It is undeniable today that Christian mentalities have adjusted to a more accurate reading of the New Testament, and thus rediscovered that what Jesus preached was rooted in the Jewish culture of his time and in the biblical tradition. Ample evidence of this can be found in the recent writings of numerous Jewish scholars on the subject.

When Christians read the Bible as they value, respect, and love it, they then form a highly religious picture of the Jews and of Israel. The conflicts between the Jewish and Christian interpretations of the Scriptures may remain tense. They may have degenerated into fratricidal, too often deadly persecutions. Yet, such confrontations now no longer ignore that the other is the closest brother. Christian attitudes have been purified by gestures of repentance, supplications for forgiveness, and prayers at the Wailing Wall. Pope John Paul has clearly identified his "elder brothers."

It would hardly be an exaggeration to say that the devout Christian is not far from considering any Jew as a reminder of the prophetic word or as a bearer of the sacred features of the history of salvation.

Looking for Partners

In the second place, as far as the Jewish religion is concerned, a Catholic will be tempted to picture it in the image of his own ecclesial institutions. This is the case especially in France, where the Napoleonic emancipation (later extended to the rest of the Old Continent) has structured Judaism on the model of Catholicism, the latter as "the religion of the majority of the French." As a result, rabbis are considered to be like priests and synagogues like churches — or, rather, they are placed at the same level.

Such equation of respective practices and rites has projected on Judaism the way Catholics understand themselves. This is why they can be dumbfounded when finding out, even when they are learned, that *cohanim* or *leviim* need not be rabbis, and vice versa.

Thirdly, the historic evolution of Catholic mentalities has led to differentiating religious from political authorities. Such a distinction is familiar to Jewish culture. However, the result is that members of the Catholic hierarchy, when they look for partners, will spontaneously see rabbis or great rabbis as their religious counterparts. Unless they are very well informed, they will tend to underestimate or take as strictly political the other institutional forms of Jewish life and identity. This may account for the (understandable) difficulty for them today to grasp the true nature of the State of Israel or of such an organization as yours.

The Jew as Stranger

Fourthly, it is easy to guess that what is most confusing for Christians is the Jewish identity. You may object that this is a bone of contention as well among Jews themselves. But that does not prevent anyone from being aware of what is at stake.

So what do Einstein, Cohn-Bendit, Marx, Freud, Ben Gurion, Rosenzweig, Buber, Rabin, Begin, Bergson, or Mendelssohn and countless others have in common, except that they are Jewish? Yet, what does that mean? Is it a feeling of unparalleled strangeness? Or is it the intuition of a subtle link, blending repressed recollections with the slogans of anti-Semitism? This is what sometimes leads non-Jews to ask the most naïve — and sometimes hurtful — questions.

Jewish strangeness is made even stronger by the concrete situation of the Jewish populations, who have experienced perpetual migrations along the centuries. A Jew will hardly ever or only rarely be considered as a true native in any European country. After several generations, he virtually always remains an immigrant, and thus a stranger, and even more so because of his unmistakably distinct religion or identity.

Finally, the Shoah cannot be omitted. It is what sets today's Jews indelibly apart. Non-Jews see it as the distinctive mark which triggers the shameful horror of guilt and the terror of a threatening prophecy. All this only strengthens the both fascinating and disturbing features of Jewishness in the Christian consciousness.

A Common Destiny

In short, what Christians are at a loss to take hold of is the Jewish identity. And yet, such institutions as the Crif in France, or the European Jewish Congress, or your World Jewish Congress bear witness to it. Whatever their religious, cultural, political, or ideological diversity, and whatever their theoretical differences when it comes to defining themselves, all Jews have something in common. Moreover, this common identity resists all criticisms and attempts or temptations to drift apart.

It is not linked to any nationality, or culture, or language. It is not even dependent upon religious practice, although this has played and still plays a key role traditionally.

It is rather the awareness of an indelible common destiny, implying a certain ideal in human life.

It is the remembrance (even if it is buried) of several millennia of a history dominated by dispersion and persecutions, and at the same time the hope indestructibly rooted in the promise of life.

It is also the notion of a duty towards life and humanity.

As long as a non-Jew, whether Catholic or not, fails to catch a glimpse of this reality, he will find it hard to relate to the Jewish world. In a certain way, the difficulty also concerns the birth and existence of the State of Israel. We know that its recognition was a decisive step toward a normal relationship between the Catholic Church and the Jewish world.

In Symmetry . . .

Now the symmetrical picture of the way Jews see Catholics will only underline how difficult mutual recognition actually is.

Firstly, it would be simplistic to answer with only one word: "They're just *goyim*," for that term remains somewhat ambiguous.

Among *Ashkenazim*, it used to be synonymous with "Christian," since the non-Jewish population who lived alongside were Christian by definition. In that case, the Jewish consciousness in its turn projected on others its own identification standards.

Yet, there is some weakness in this approach, as diversity is infinitely greater among non-Jews than it is within Judaism. Hardly any consistency can be found outside Judaism, except locally, on the basis of national or religious belonging, or of a cultural or professional tradition. It is a widespread misconception in the Jewish universe to describe the rest of the world as falling into only one category.

Secondly, at the religious level, for many centuries the Jewish tradition has chosen to ignore the fact of Christianity, and even to avoid simply naming it. When the issue was raised, the answer usually was that Jews had no need of Christians to understand themselves. This may be true when it comes to defining the essence of Judaism. It is less evident, however, in describing the destiny of Israel and its fecundity in the course of time. In any case, such an answer does not allow to account for the paths that have been followed by the peoples whose history has been shaped by the Bible they had received from the Jews.

An Incurable Disease

In the third place, the weight of history has made the relationship between Jews and non-Jews ambivalent in the West, both with efforts to identify with or even assimilate Judaism, and efforts to reject or even eliminate it. Jews remember their marginal and enslaved condition, while Catholics would rather forget it. Moreover, the liberties that have been progressively granted in the logic of emancipation since the Age of Enlightenment have tended to erase the Jewish specificity and to replace it by a common identity based on rational citizenship.

Although Jews have often played a decisive part in the shaping of modern culture, their difference has remained. Its origins may have become mysterious. It may even have disappeared as Jews themselves became oblivious to their strangeness. But it has always been present or capable of reemerging, if need be, paradoxically, under the threat of an incurable disease, one of the names of which is anti-Semitism. As soon as anti-Judaism manifests itself, it will awaken in Jewish memories the remembrance, or even the reminiscence of recollections, of persecutions, stakes, the Inquisition, ghettoes, pogroms, and camps. Such indelible images of the past weigh tremendously upon our thoughts and choices, but no more than the determination and strength to see to the triumph of life.

The Truth of Dialogue

This is why it is necessary to carry on the patient labor of mutual recognition, so as to grasp how Jews and Catholics truly see each other. We have to come to terms with the legacy that both unites and divides us.

We have to know the other, both emotionally and concretely, if genuine dialogue is to overcome suspicions and wounded sensitiveness.

As I look back over the past twenty years, when I found myself in a privileged position to observe both sides, I cannot but admire the dedication and perseverance with which a number of both Jewish leaders and Catholic officials have struggled to rise above the misgivings and criticisms generated by the blows of the past, by the aggressive defensiveness inherited from centuries of persecutions and contempt.

On the other hand, when trust is shared, it becomes possible to speak out in truth and in depth, out of accepted mutual esteem and respect, as sensible beings belonging to one and the same human family. The real nature of the disagreements may then appear authentically, untainted by the confrontations of the past or by fears for the future.

I want to insist: the goal is not simply to reach the ideal of consensus or just successful communication. But we have to become aware of sensitivities, of their histories, of convictions, of silences, and even of what remains ignored.

Such a work requires personal relationships, while in the developed countries social life does not always encourage open, direct debates, and rather continually unearths fresh bones of contention.

For us, anti-Semitism remains a nagging challenge. The Zionist bet offered a radical solution by giving to the Jewish condition of the Diaspora the identity of a nation that could defend itself and make itself respected. Another option banks on people's rights and common rationality, as is the case with the French legislation, which exposes and punishes anti-Semitism as a crime.

These reactions to recurrent expressions of anti-Judaism have their merits as well as their limits. For anti-Semitism is the exasperated consequence of the denial of our difference — that unique difference which characterizes the Jewish condition, a difference that remains unmatched because it rests on the Election of Israel.

Dealing with such irrational, symbolic power, which may be subverted into destructive violence, calls for wisdom and prudence. This is exactly where trustful dialogue between Catholic and Jewish representatives can contribute to containing senseless outbursts of resentment or vengeance, and — with God's help — to opening up respectful debates and fruitful exchanges.

Convergences

Getting together and knowing each other better, however, will not be enough to wipe out all disagreements. But — and this is the second stage of this address — such dialogue should — or rather will — allow us to point out the convergences that cultural globalization is likely to facilitate nowadays. Mutual understanding will also foster a new awareness of shared perspectives on key aspects of social life.

Beyond Ideology

Beyond our numerous shortcomings, the first vision we have in common is an ethical one. Of course, a great diversity can be found among Jews as well as among Christians concerning the norms of human behavior. Nevertheless, the fact is that the message of the Bible and that of the Gospel strongly and really converge on ethical issues, as has been verified in many circumstances, even despite the hazards of ideology. Two words may sum up this ethical attitude: *justice* and *peace*. The towering figure of René Cassin, who was the principal writer of the Declaration of Human Rights proclaimed in Paris in 1948, remains a dazzling example of this convergence.

At this level, it is not without interest to recall the role played by Jews in the genesis and evolution of Marxism. A number of us adopted it, out of a passionate love of justice. And the same individuals, or their children, found themselves on the front line when it came to challenging dictatorships or terror in order to defend human dignity. They have paid a heavy price for such resistance.

Perhaps my viewpoint is too religious, or simply unduly optimistic? What remains anyway is that, whenever the human condition is concerned, with all it implies at the level of legislation, Christian and

Jewish representatives prove to agree on the principles and foundations of social life.

Religious Liberty as the Key to Democracy

Another common point between the experience at the root of the Jewish identity and the Christian faith or the cultures it may have inspired, is a certain idea of democracy and liberty.

The preservation of individual rights and of political freedom is part of the Jewish tradition, as criticisms of the monarchy are part of the biblical revelation, while such royal figures as David or Solomon are idealized.

The Christian tradition took up the same approach, although empires were also attempting to use Christianity to sacralize their rule and were therefore logically tempted simultaneously to persecute Jews. Nowadays, the defense of religious liberty leads us both to deny the state any sacred authority or control of human conscience, because such power can only be God's.

Perhaps, again, my vocabulary is too religious to deal with the political problem of citizenship? What remains, once more, is that today the Jewish experience and the Catholic tradition agree to maintain that what is sacred or religious belongs in the most intimate heart of the conscience of man as "image and resemblance of God," and in personal worship of the truth.

The confessional or ethnic particularities which make up the treasure of each human identity should not be rubbed out by democratic equality. The latter should rather open up the social space that is necessary for everyone to live with his or her distinctive characteristics while respecting the liberty of others and caring for the common good.

The fact is that, in today's world, Jewish communities thrive in countries with a Christian culture, where democracy is best established, that is to say Western Europe and the United States of America.

Universalism and Communion

One third (and practical) point is decisively relevant in the social sphere. It can be described by a word that has virtually become trivial: *racism*.

From a Jewish point of view, the difference between Israel and the nations is not determined by ethnic or cultural factors. But it is rooted exclusively in the remembrance of the founding call that gave to the Jewish people a mission in the service of all. No human superiority or inferiority is significant in the eyes of the Most High. Only the relationship to the Holy One creates a distinction that carries universal hope and the seeds of equal rights for all.

The Christian approach has been undermined from within by national identities. But in the wake of Israel's universalism, Christianity is aware of carrying the promise of a universal communion. Each culture, ethnic group, language, or nation deserves to be recognized in its specificity, but none can claim to be superior or to assert a supremacy that would inevitably offend the common dignity and the unique vocation of all.

Moreover, the design of divine Providence, as Catholicism understands it from the Bible, is to gather all human families. They already share the same origin, which they received from their Creator. They are called to share the same blessing in the promise made through Abraham to all nations.

If the State of Israel was condemned as "racist" by the United Nations in 1975, for the same reason as the South Africa of apartheid, it must have been in ignorance of the Lord's ways and of the Election of his people — as if the sacred distinction between Israel and the nations had been abolished, and could deceitfully be reduced to an alleged *"limpieza di sangre."*

In truth, the Catholic notion of communion is inspired by that of the people of God and of the relationship between Israel and the *goyim*. The temptation that Catholicism has experienced has been that of the pagans, that is to say, to eliminate the uniqueness of Israel from its consciousness. The risk for Jews is to consign all the nations to some threatening mist, and to ignore Christianity if the latter cannot be forgotten.

Perhaps common reflections will allow both to refine their perceptions and to improve their practices?

Knowing Oneself Better When Facing the Other

To conclude, I wish to add a remark which concerns the domain of faith more directly.

The legacy of past polemics and suspicions has left frozen irritations among Christians as well as among Jews, in the way they see both themselves and the others. At the intellectual level, this has too often led not exactly to denying the other but — to borrow a medical term — to scotomize him or, shall we say, to act as if he did not exist.

Dialogue allows us to reinitiate a relationship, but it also forces each partner to reconsider himself in front of the other, and thus to change, and even to renew himself in the course of the exchange.

On the Catholic side, thanks to Israel, now Hebrew is better known, as the language of the Bible, along with all the wealth of the Jewish tradition that has commented upon it. Dramatic technological improvements in transportation have also made the land of Israel itself more accessible, with all its history, and Catholic consciousness has discovered and assimilated much of this reality in the last fifty years. That land now has become almost familiar to many rank-and-file church-goers, while biblical scholars can now make the most of immediate experiences as they study the texts of the Scriptures and the events of sacred history.

More deeply, the recognition of the State of Israel and of the Lord's irrevocable gift to his people has prompted Catholics to rediscover where the salvation they believe in comes from, and to acknowledge the fecundity of these origins. The way the Church understands herself has been refashioned along the lines of the too often forgotten vision of the economy of salvation provided by the Scriptures of both the Old and the New Testaments.

Is it possible to imagine that a similar, symmetrical movement could take place on the Jewish side?

The specialists of Qumran and of early Christianity know how lively and diversified Jewish thinking can be in this field, and how freely the issues are discussed. Would it be utopian to hope for regenerated, positive, benevolent dialogues between Christians as such and Jews as such, in faithfulness to each tradition, so as to allow spiritual breakthroughs whose rewards cannot be determined beforehand?

In other words, I am ready to bet on a fecundity of which we can only have a vague intuition today. Perhaps we shall have to wait until the next generation, given the pressure of the outside world, for such exchanges to take place and to be seen by all those involved not as threats to their respective identities, but as opportunities to strengthen and develop them.

Rethinking Our Common Vocation

Examining, as we are doing now, how Jews and Catholics look at each other and what they may converge on in the world that is taking shape does not merely amount to teaming up for some tactical purpose. It is rather acknowledging that God's Spirit is at work in history, and helping one another better to understand our destiny.

Meeting with Christianity does unveil something of the Jewish vocation by revealing some of the fruits the latter has borne. In such encounters grafts prove to have been made on the Jewish root. They may seem foreign to it, but they guarantee its everlastingness and they testify to its origin. They are opportunities for Israel to rediscover its call to universality.

Not without suspicions, struggles, and tragedies, such immense exchanges have already begun at the secular level of modern humanism. Our task now is to explore the full dimensions of Israel's vocation, from its indelible origin to its promised accomplishment.

CHAPTER 15

What Do Christian-Jewish Encounters Mean as Civilizations Clash?

The phrase "clash of civilizations," as Mr. Huntington coined it, has been rather widely brushed aside in Europe, much in the same way as one strives to exorcise some bewitchment. It seemed politically harmful to let public opinion picture the world as caught in some kind of a new binary antagonism. Europe has kept on waging civil wars in the past centuries, and remains wary of simplistic binary confrontations.

In order to argue rationally, I suggest that we take for granted here not a "clash of civilizations" but a total recomposition of global civilization, with scores of conflicts and disagreements, also with heaps of convergences and exchanges as well as defensive withdrawals — in short, a stage where everything is wonderfully bubbling up.

In such a situation one immediately perceives the momentousness of good neighborly relationships between Christians and Jews, between Jewish organizations, or the religious representatives of Judaism, and Catholic officials, between the Holy See and the State of Israel.

Address to the American Jewish Committee, Washington, D.C., May 8, 2002. Translated by Jean Duchesne.

Problematics

However, do new, positive, trustful relations merely point to common interests, economic coordination, and the cooperation that is required for two partners to defend their respective identities by facing adversity together? As you must guess, this is not the way I see such a connection, either in its principle, or when examining the reasons for its renewal, or (above all) when considering its significance for the future and service of all civilizations — or (better) of all that civilization implies.

I then propose that we follow the problematics I am now going to outline by raising five queries:

1. What do Jews and Christians have in common that may justify their getting closer to each other, and becoming allies?
2. As Jews and Christians acknowledge what they have in common, will their respective characteristics and identities be threatened by such companionship?
3. Does this common principle mean anything for humankind as a whole?
4. Do both Jews and Christians become better able, when they get together, to carry out their specific mission with regard to the rest of humankind?
5. Finally, if such caring for the world does not reflect any ambition to conquer or dominate, how can this universalism express itself concretely?

My approach may sound disturbingly typical of French Cartesian logic. So I have a deal to offer: what about taking these queries in reverse order? That's the way the best negotiators manage to work out a satisfactory outcome!

The Biblical Model

So let us begin with the fifth and last question: if the universalism that Jews and Christians have in common serves no purpose of conquest, how can it manifest itself practically for the good of humanity?

The answer will be: through an original approach and practice of political action.

In biblical history, the only obvious political achievement was the kingdom of David and Solomon, even though what followed did not keep the promises. . . . If you take a look at the various nations where Jews live, you won't find many of them at the helm. They have been prime ministers at best, like Benjamin Disraeli in Britain, or Léon Blum in France.

In fact, the biblical model that Jews may refer to when it comes to dealing with political affairs would rather be Mordecai, the adviser. His wisdom and intelligence are inspired by his faithfulness and obedience to God, and this allows him to make judicious, reasonable suggestions to a sovereign who does not himself belong to the Jewish people or share its creed.

You may object that Queen Esther ought to be taken into account as well. Granted. But this can be reserved for the Purim festival!

Now what do we find on the Catholic side? There is no doubt that the hordes of sovereigns who claimed to be Catholics wanted to rule not only their nations but also the Church. And yet, in fidelity to the biblical tradition and to the teachings of the New Testament, Catholicism itself does not demand political control of the nations or the peoples. Just remember Jesus' answer about the tax levied by the Romans: "Render therefore to Caesar the things that are Caesar's, and to God the things that are God's" (Matthew 22:21).

Ethics and Politics

However, is it adequate to speak of biblical and Catholic influences or inspirations? Some might fancy that two lobbies, one Jewish, the other

Christian, are at work together so as to defend their mutual special interests. This is not at all what I have in mind!

What I mean is rather a common vocation to both advise and criticize "the prince," and to challenge the temptation of absolutism. This concerns not merely the fascination with tyranny, and no less the inducement, which is inherent in any power (since political rulers also make the laws), to set oneself up as the judge of good and evil.

Now this is exactly where Jews and Christians share one same clear principle. It is that the law that imposes itself on human conscience comes from a source much higher than any man. What is good does not depend upon wishes or opinions, but imposes itself as an absolute in this world where all is relative. And it is this indisputable norm in temporal affairs which makes of politics a reality that is worthy of human destiny.

Such an ethical approach to politics inherently calls any arbitrariness into question. Its aim is to enlighten the exercise of power, not to destroy it. The goal is to testify to genuine wisdom, which comes from God as the Bible teaches us.

This is a truly high human ideal. The position of the Jewish people and of Christians as watchers of and witnesses to God's reign is a protest that undermines any human dominion. Are we not, Jews and Christians together, responsible and accountable to humanity as a whole for this political principle?

Is this not precisely the kind of wisdom that is missing in international organizations? They have been set up to regulate peace among the nations. But their efficiency is limited by conflicting forces and interests, which hardly allow them to meet the requirements of justice and moral law (see Genesis 18:18).

What I am saying may sound utopian. Yet, I can mention one fact, and ask: is this not what Pope John Paul II has been relentlessly striving to achieve for more than twenty years? Has he not been successful sometimes? Perhaps you might remember as well the key role played by "dear Henry" in world politics a few decades ago. But I don't want to interfere in the American scene, and I leave this to your appreciation.

From the Law to Love

Let us now come to the next question: when Jews and Christians meet, does this allow them to carry out their specific mission in the service of the whole of humankind?

To answer, we should meditate upon the gift of the Law, or the Commandments.

On the Jewish side first: even if he is a legal expert or a specialist of the history of the Roman or Anglo-Saxon juridical system, no Jew can come across the word *law* without thinking of the Torah. If we leave aside here the question of the implementation of precepts as detailed by the rabbinical tradition, we can focus on the wisdom of the Law and its power over human conscience. What matters is not the sanction that comes along with the rule, but the justice that is thus established in human relationships. In every one of its aspects, and even this is invisible most of the time, the Law is based on God's holy will as it was revealed on Mount Sinai. In some way or other, the Law receives from God a sacred character, which also concerns man, to whom it is destined.

Now what about Christians? Perhaps I will surprise those among you who know little about the Catholic doctrine, no matter whether they are Christians or Jews, by recalling that, in substance, the biblical commandments are received by Christians as God's revelation, given in the Old Testament.

You can take a look at the most recent document that makes this clear: the *Catechism of the Catholic Church,* published under the authority of Pope John Paul II. Morals are presented within the frame of the Ten Commandments, which structure the development of the ethical reflection on personal and social human behavior.

Of course, as disciples of Jesus, we differ in the way we understand these commandments and put them into practice. For a Christian, the authorized interpretation of God's Word is the way Jesus obeyed them, and asks us to observe them.

This comprehension is a determined adherence to the "*Shema, Israel:* Love the Lord your God with all your heart, with all your soul, and

159

with all your might," of both Deuteronomy (6:4-5) and the Gospel according to Matthew (22:37). The first rule of action sums up the Law and the Prophets with the double commandment of the love of God and of the neighbor, as found in both Leviticus (19:18) and Matthew (22:37-39), so as to imitate and participate in the love received from the Messiah: "Love one another as I have loved you," as John puts it in his Gospel (15:12).

Vigilance and Testimony: A Common Mission

It would be shortsighted to declare that the gap between the two interpretations cannot be bridged. A more accurate look will allow discerning that they have a common source — in God. The consequences for human comportment are the same, even when justice and peace materialize along distinct lines and are welcomed by tapping specific spiritual resources. Of course, the dissimilitudes should not be overlooked. They are even essential to each experience. And yet, the moral convergence between Jews and Christians allows them to carry out their mission toward humankind, through vigilance and testimony.

Can the tasks be divided up between the ones and the others? That would be presumptuous and probably mistaken, since this is a domain where everything is interrelated and nothing can be isolated.

The Christian experience may have led at times, among certain believers, to some relativization of the Commandments in the name of charity. It goes without saying that the love of God and of the neighbor fully sums up the Law. No precept can be more accurate, stronger or more beautiful. What remains, however, is that the demands of love must absolutely be strictly interpreted and structured by the respect of God's will. It might be fruitful to remind some Christians that they should not forget what God explicitly asks for, and some Jews that the commandment of love at the beginning of *Shema, Israel* is meant to inspire all the attitudes that claim to obey it, in human relationships as well as toward God.

Christian universalism has offered to all the nations of the world, sometimes under secularized forms, what has been given to Israel on Sinai. Israel remains the guarantor of that gift, together with Christians, without doubt, for the greater good of all humankind.

"All the Nations on Earth"

This leads me to the next query: as Jews and Christians get closer to each other, what does this mean for all men?

I am obviously not going to answer by measuring the impact of such a prospect on public opinion. Some will fear the result might be a threat to the independence and liberty of national or religious particular identities. Others (or perhaps the same) will also wonder how two religions which have been so drastically separated in history could establish any special relationship that would be capable of bringing all cultures and creeds together.

As a matter of fact, this link with humanity as a whole is inscribed in the very origin of Judaism. Remember the blessing of Abraham in Genesis (12:3): "By you all the nations of the earth shall bless themselves." You may also recall the prophecy of Isaiah (2:2-3) according to which "all the nations shall flow to the mountain of the LORD, to the house of the God of Jacob, that he may teach [them] his ways and that [they] may walk in his paths."

Among Christians, the Jewish apostles of Jesus strove, not without much difficulty, to actualize this prophecy, as they discovered, almost despite themselves, that the gift of the Spirit that had been promised to Israel was also granted to the pagans. When Jesus ordered his followers, as Matthew reports (28:19) it, to "go therefore and make disciples of all nations, baptizing them . . . and teaching them to observe all [he had] commanded," in reality he united Christians to Jews in their hope for the world — even if the respective spiritual attitudes and experiences could remain different.

For the Jewish people is in a paradoxical situation. It still is a people and keeps on claiming this quality. The question whether it is a people like the others or different from them has been asked since its origins. We are a people unlike all other nations, because we have been chosen by God to serve him. And we are a nation similar to the others when it comes to asking for a king or struggling for power as anywhere else in the world. This old tension has resurfaced in the Diaspora since the creation of the State of Israel. What is left is that, with today's globalization, the Jews and Jewish communities spread all over the world genuinely take part in the diversity of cultures and nations, while their belonging to "the Jewish people" is no less certain for it.

In the same way, it can be said that the fact of being Christian incorporates every person and community into the common life of the Messiah's Church, which is present across all the stages of history, in all nations and all cultures.

Unity and Unicity

The problem I am trying to tackle here is the one raised by globalization. Is humanity today actually linked in any solidarity? Is the price to pay the denial or oblivion of the specificities that used to be considered assets but may now be seen as relics from the past and obstacles? Of course not.

But the mission given by God's Word to Jews and then to Christians is to make humankind aware of its unity and of its unique vocation, which comes from its origin. As the first page of Genesis (1:26) puts it, man was created by God "in his image and resemblance." Within the human diversity, there exist watchers of and witnesses to the light of the origin. Their job is not to impose anything, but to help humankind decipher its destiny.

The Jews are conscious of their historical singularity, since this Revelation was entrusted to them first, once and for all. It was in the experience of a people shaped by this Election that sacred history took flesh in human history. The temptation that the Jewish people have to face, then, is obviously to lock themselves up in this uniqueness, and thus to deprive it of its saving significance.

Christians benefit from the first blessing, since pagans were blessed in their turn when the Church was born, and they were thus granted to share in the Promise. In the course of history, Christians have been tempted, too, to create new singularities of a national or confessional kind. But they then lost the sense of their roots and of the origin that guarantees their hope.

When they meet and size up their differences, Jews and Christians can grasp better what is given to them as both founding evidence and a vital task: to convey to divided men the call to a unity that is greater and stronger than their enormous diversity.

A Necessary Encounter

Our next point is that evoking such prospects is no threat to Jewish specificity or to Christian identity.

Let us try to clarify this. In John's Gospel (4:22), Jesus teaches to a Samaritan woman that "Salvation is from the Jews."

If there were no Jews, Christian universality might melt away into some abstract humanism. But the mission entrusted to Christians is based on the faith that cultural diversity can be respected, in spite of sometimes impressive difficulties and ambiguities, and that each culture can be enhanced by acknowledging the unity of humankind, as the child of the Only God.

If there were no Christians, could Judaism carry out its specific mission as the bearer of the blessing promised to all nations without being absorbed into the universal rationality of Enlightenment, without depriving of its substance the history that has begotten it?

The lesson we can draw from these aporias is that closer relations between Jews and Christians are necessary to both for each side to grasp what God may be demanding from it. Both what is common in their experiences and their differences in interpreting God's blessing sketch out a picture of the unity of the universal communion that is rooted in the Promise made to Abraham, as it was announced by the Prophets, and as it is attested to by the Catholic Church, in the humble boldness of her faith.

All this may seem exaggerated to you, but it points to a challenge that we all have to take up in these times of globalization.

On the one hand, what is the Jewish identity? Is it the national Israeli identity, or the diasporic identity? What is it grounded on?

On the other hand, is the Christian universalistic message nothing but the mask of an imperialism that used to be Roman and now is Occidental? How can this message be spread across the cultures of the world without losing its strength or dissolving its contents? The problem becomes all the more acute when Christians carry the biblical message, including the Torah, to such nations as those of Asia, and when the latter declare that they are ready, as Gandhi was, to welcome what Jesus Christ said as a liberation, but claim they can do without the Bible, since they have their own scriptures and sacred history. Christianity is lost if it accepts to be uprooted from Israel, that is to say from the Covenant, from God's fundamental choice.

The relationship, or the link, between Jews and Christians, with the tension between them that will always have to be respected, is what gives all of humanity its original face, and encourages its hope for unity in peace.

A Break within the First Christian Generation

What is then the justification for Jews and Christians getting closer? What do they have in common that may provide grounds for an alliance? This is our last question, at the top of the list.

The answer is written on the first page of the New Testament. If you open any translation of the Gospels, you will find it begins with a genealogy: "Abraham was the father of Isaac, and Isaac the father of Jacob, and Jacob the father of Judah and his brothers. . . ." These lines are the opening of what Matthew (1:1-2), the first evangelist, calls "the genealogy of Jesus Christ, the son of David, the son of Abraham."

A Christian receives from the Jewish people the totality of the Holy Scripture: the Law, the Prophets, and all the other writings. And we receive it as it is: the Word of God. And this is true of all Christians

— Protestants, Catholics, and Orthodox alike — whatever their crimes and the trials of history. And this Holy Scripture cannot be separated from the ones to whom it was first addressed, or from the languages in which it was originally worded. The Church receives each and every of these statements as inspired by God's Spirit. She wants to be faithful to them. She even claims she cannot survive without them, while some (like Marcion in the second century) insisted on breaking away radically, and removing from the faith of Jesus' disciples all the biblical documents, and with them the Covenant and the Election.

Now have there not been symmetrical attempts at reduction on the Jewish side? The motivations may remain only too obvious to all of us and it would not help much to recall them here. The point is that silence became the rule. Too many Jews argued in the past that they had no need of Christians at the religious level.

In fact, we can recognize in these contradictory attitudes the internal rupture that took place within the first Christian generation, as Jews either refused or accepted the message of Jesus of Nazareth.

Differences and Communion in Hope

Jews and Christians or Catholics thus share both a common root and a conflict. But from a Christian point of view, this conflict has a background that is familiar to Jewish thought, in the expectation of the accomplishment of history according to God's will.

Christians as well as Jews bank on the same hope. The Revelation that they have received and that they transmit turns their eyes toward the achievement whose features are shaped on each side by the experiences of centuries, cultures, and nations, and also by whatever is accepted or refused from the other.

Who does not feel here that the tensions may be all the more incisive and painful as the reasons for agreement and communion are indelible? Since we share the same roots, any hostility will be felt as the blow of a wound, or as a denial. But misunderstandings can also be seen in the light of even greater hope.

When we look back at history today, and even if renewed closeness cannot erase the differences, the urgency of the original call forces the separated brothers, the elder one and the younger one, to undertake, each one for his part, the mission that has been given to him. Neither can fulfill it without the other, or by forcing him or ignoring him.

Today's figure of humankind somehow anticipates, through obscurities and contradictions, the hope offered by the Prophets and proclaimed by the New Testament. It would be an illusion and a lie to overlook what may divide us and to ignore each person's faith so as to make the common hope a reality. That would be a mistake, or, in truth, an abdication. But every one is called to progress in the work of justice and peace that has been assigned to him by the divine Providence.

The common link between Jews and Christians is the source of their alliance. It guarantees the mission they have to carry out, unless they choose to take the risk of betraying humanity. The stakes are no less than the balance and peace of the world.

Two Sensitive Points

To conclude, I want to insist that the biblical Revelation, as the Jewish tradition receives it, and as the Church accepts it through her faith in Christ, is a treasure that remains to be explored for the benefit of the future of humankind.

If exchanges can develop in mutual trust and closeness between faithful, considerate men and women, how enriching it may become for Christian thought to welcome the Election of Israel as a fundamental datum of human history and of the Church's vocation! Moreover, as mutual understanding between Jews and Christians is gradually established, their common approach to biblical history may allow a wiser grasp of the diversity of religious practices and cultures. A few months ago in Assisi, the Pope showed the way.

With the Election, Redemption seems to me to be another key issue. For two millennia Jewish reflection has been very wary of chapters 42 to 53 of Isaiah, as though they had been monopolized by Christians.

However, how is it possible not to discuss together, without ruling out anything beforehand, sin, suffering, the hope for salvation, the repentance that is expected from man, God's forgiveness, and the contents of what we are looking forward to?

The fear of hurting one another, of wanting to get the better of each other, as was the case in the *disputationes* of past centuries, must not bury the prophetic word of Isaiah at a time when the nations yearn for happiness ever more explicitly, even though there is a growing awareness of impending calamities; at a time when risks and fears seem never to have been greater because of the new powers that men have acquired.

Joint Heirs

On these two most sensitive points — the Election, and Redemption — only a fresh dialogue between Christians and Jews will allow us to catch a glimpse of the light given by God to his people and promised to all the nations.

The common future for Jews and Catholics cannot be reduced to eliminating as many bones of contention as possible. Neither will peaceful mutual understanding be enough, or even solidarity in the service of humanity. For such a future calls for work on what separates us as well as on what we have in common. May differences and tensions become a stimulus to reach ever deeper, carefully and obediently, into the mystery of which history makes us the joint heirs!

Jews and Christians are to get closer for the service of humanity, so that they may foster peace and be sources of blessings for all.

Afterword

Translated by Jean Duchesne

T he English edition of this book deserves a special afterword, in which I would like, with hindsight, to develop some of the brief reflections expressed in my foreword.

Speaking Out or Keeping Silent

I must first come back to one fact that may astonish the younger generations: until the mid 1970s the victims or witnesses of the Shoah were locked up in the incapability of speaking out. How can we account for their silence? Does such speechlessness have anything in common with that of the same generations in both East and West Germany? I could not say. In any case, the parallelism does not provide an explanation for either muteness.

As far as the silence of the Jews is concerned — and this is something I myself have experienced — it is rooted in the feeling — I dare not call it the memory or the consciousness — of an unspeakable, unfathomable tragedy. Speaking out was impossible. Any word sent one back into the abyss. One did not refuse to speak out; one simply was unable to. Only those who shared this suffering can understand each other without saying anything.

That silence on the ordeal is that of the Lamb described by Isaiah (53:7). It has nothing to do with passive, irresponsible cowardice in face of crime.

In 1979, the cultural environment — the *kairos* — was changing. Speaking out about what was first called the Holocaust, then the Shoah, was eventually becoming possible. Yet, I would certainly not have accepted the invitation of the nuns at Sainte Françoise Romaine if they had asked me to lecture about "the mystery of Israel," even in the sense already proposed by Erik Peterson or Jacques Maritain. Indeed, I did not yet feel ready to express the thoughts I had nurtured for so many years. But they requested me to preach a retreat, and that was quite another matter, so I gladly agreed.

It should be remembered that the first (and larger) part of this book is a commentary of the Gospel according to Saint Matthew, intended to nourish the prayer of contemplative nuns. It is a meditation of the divine Word as it resonates in the silence of the abyss that I have just mentioned. The divine Word then triggers echoes, whispers and explosions that otherwise cannot be heard.

I did not use the Gospel according to Saint Matthew to deal with the mystery of Israel. Rather it was the Gospel itself, as it was reread and meditated upon, which led and even forced me to tackle the mystery of Israel and the nations for the sake of the women who were listening to me and whose vocation is prayer. This mystery appeared to me as the light that "cannot be hidden under a bushel."

Indeed, those notions were not new to me. I had discovered and admired the way Gaston Fessard, S.J., had developed into a theology of history Saint Paul's threefold assertion in Galatians 3:28: "There is neither Jew nor Greek, there is neither slave nor free, there is neither male nor female; for you are all one in Christ Jesus." But I had learned at my own expense what truth is expressed in Jesus' warning to his disciples when he quotes Isaiah (6:9-10) to explain to them why he speaks in parables, and how reluctant man remains in his heart to welcome him (Matthew 13:10-15): "To you it has been given to know the secrets of the kingdom of Heaven, but to them it has not been given. . . . This is why I speak to them in parables, because seeing they do not see, and hearing they do not hear, nor do they understand. With them indeed is fulfilled the prophecy of Isaiah which says: 'You shall indeed hear but never understand, and you shall indeed see but never perceive. For this people's heart has grown dull, and their ears are heavy of hearing, and their eyes they have closed, lest they should perceive with their eyes, and hear with their ears, and understand with their heart, and turn for me to heal them.'"

It was my experience that few Christians — be they believers or not — were ready to accept this dimension of the mystery of salvation that is announced in Christ's Gospel. And until then, I had followed Jesus' advice. I hope not to offend anyone as I quote it now. Toward the end of the Sermon on the Mount, Jesus says (according to Matthew 7:6): "Do not give dogs what is holy; do not throw your pearls before swine, lest they trample them under foot and turn to attack you." You know that the dogs here, as in the story of the Canaanite woman, represent the pagans to whom the mystery of God has not been revealed. Similarly, the pigs are the animals which symbolize the pagans' relationship with death.

Jesus' advice certainly does not mean that one should shrink from announcing the Gospel to the pagan nations. But it does ask us to take into account the divine mercy that opens hearts and minds when the time has come. When these nuns invited me, I felt the need to share what little God had given me to discover of his treasures and pearls.

It was thus God's Word, shared with contemplative nuns, which guided this meditation on the consolation of Israel in the spirit of the filial freedom (cf. Matthew 17:26) "for [which] Christ has set us free" (Galatians 5:1). Yet that Word must be shared with care, lest it may hurt Rachel "weeping for her children; she refused to be consoled, because they were no more" (Matthew 2:18).

This is the reason why for many years I could not allow these pages to be published.

If I eventually accepted in 2002, it was — as I explained in the foreword — because of the gift made to the Church and to the world through the ministry of John Paul II after the Second Vatican Council. This is why I chose for the cover of the French edition of the book the picture on which the Pope can be seen inserting the text of his prayer into the Western Wall of the Jerusalem Temple. This snapshot by itself said much more on the mystery of Israel and the nations than I had been able to suggest some twenty years earlier, so that I had to agree to the publication of these meditations, as the Church herself, through Peter's successor, had opened the way, while a few thoughtful readers urged me to follow suit.

This is finally why I beg my readers, insofar as they can, to receive this meditation as what it was originally meant to be.

The Crisis of the Christian West

This second point is even more difficult to explain than the former. I have to come back to my own story, which I have so far always refused to do. If I must today, it is not because I feel the need to justify myself, but simply in order to make myself understood.

The comments that were published when this book was first released in France and in other European countries were very kind and sometimes even laudatory. But they focused mostly on the relationships between Jews and Christians, and they seemed to fail to grasp other issues, which I consider extremely important — especially the spiritual situation of the Christian West in connection with its Jewish roots. The spiritual stakes become obvious when the Catholic faith is challenged by its own children as they are confronted with modernity.

I remember my youth, just after the Second World War, when I went to university. I was eighteen, and I had been baptized only a few years earlier. I was astonished to find that my fellow students who had been born Catholics were so lukewarm, uncertain, illogical. They considered me as naively enthusiastic, and they thought that such excess was characteristic of those who were then called "converts" and are now named "catechumens."

I realized at once that this opposition between naive zeal and cautious relativism was unfair. For what was at stake was no less than the truth and content of faith. Ten years of higher education in philosophy and theology allowed me to become thoroughly acquainted with the major works of Christian Tradition and of Western modernity, and to find there, along with challenges that sometimes cannot be met adequately, the living sources of faith, where reason can be nurtured and comforted. That sufficed to commit my freedom unequivocally in answer to God's call.

And this spiritual commitment — a commitment through faith — cast its light upon the events of history. Let me simply mention here a handful of books which were decisive for my spiritual struggle: Father Henri de Lubac's *The Drama of Atheistic Humanism*, and Father Gaston Fessard's *France, Beware You Don't Lose Your Soul* and *France, Beware You Don't Lose Your Liberty*.

The landmarks I had found there allowed me to sail through the storms of the 1970s as they were shaking both the secular and the clerical intelligentsias in France. The Church was badly undermined. Many broke away and left, but also most Christians had to bear the burden of intellectual challenges for which they had not been prepared. Above all, any serious reflection was being swept away by a pervasive sociology of power, which in many cases mortally wounded the Catholics' love of the Church and trust in her.

At that time, my parish ministry gave me some time to read, pray and meditate, after fifteen busy years as Chaplain of the Sorbonne. And this crisis appeared to me as a pagan regression of Christian intelligence, with respect to the faithfulness of Israel that Jesus identifies when he encounters Nathanael (John 1:47).

It was precisely in those days, in the course of the 1970s, that I became able to overcome the silence in which I, like others, had been plunged as far as the destiny of Israel was concerned. The 1968 "revolution" was characterized by a number of sometimes delirious utopias. However, some new voices then began to make themselves heard on the intellectual scene: for example, Elie Wiesel, André Neher, Martin Buber (who was then translated into French at last), or Emmanuel Levinas (whose first books were published then).

In 1978, a year before I preached this retreat to the nuns of Sainte Françoise Romaine, Serge Klarsfeld published at his own expense his *Memorial of the Deportation of French Jews*. It is a very unusual book, basically consisting of lists of Jews sent to Auschwitz from Drancy (in the northeastern suburb of Paris, where they were first interned after they had been rounded up). Reading those very uncommon pages revealed that abyss which I have mentioned. The human weight represented by those 70,000 names invited me, as a believer and a disciple of Christ, to understand quite differently the pagan regression of Christian intelligence.

In truth, when reason disowns faith, it proves to disown itself and to lose its spiritual dimension. It is a tragic self-mutilation, because it is nothing but idolatry. The long martyrdom of Jewish faithfulness allowed me to identify this as paganism. That is what I have tried to explain in the chapter entitled "Jesus Crucified, the Messiah of Israel: Salvation for All."

Preaching this retreat to those nuns then meant for me meditating in the faith the spiritual adventure of the times. Saint Matthew's Gospel induced me to assess the faithfulness and the unfaithfulness of the Christian nations of the West in the light of the faithfulness and unfaithfulness of Israel, as the prophets give us to understand them.

My goal was not to reflect upon the place of Israel within Christian thought, for this had always seemed evident to me, ever since my first steps as a disciple of Jesus. Rather, at the end of 1978, against the background of the history of salvation where the Election of Israel plays a key role, I wanted to share my reflections on the spiritual destiny of the Christian nations of the West, on their cultural evolution and idolatrous temptations — as regards faith in Christ at the hands of the fans of demythologization, or as regards the Church, Christ's Bride, at the hands of the fans of institutional analyses. Israel had already experienced the temptation of idolatry, as the prophets' predication shows.

So perhaps it will be understood that, in those difficult years, I did receive this opportunity as God's gift, as a renewed grace, confirming and giving sense to the way along which God had led me from my birth according to the flesh, through my baptism, and to my ordination to the priesthood. This did not at all mean bearing a judgment on my contemporaries: only God can do so. I simply tried to be faithful to the light that identifies which Spirit inspires our thoughts and deeds — to that discernment that Christ evokes at the end of the Sermon on the Mount: "You will recognize them by their fruit" (Matthew 7:16).

And perhaps it will also be understood that it was no undue connection or oversimplification to put in the same bag the Shoah, the crimes of the various totalitarianisms, and the vagaries of Western culture. Finally, it should go without saying that I did not in the least mean to underestimate the legitimate demands of reason, provided the latter receives itself in the truth of the Creator's grace, of which it is the fruit.

The New York Event:
The New Conditions of Jewish-Christian Dialogue

I must also add a few remarks on the second part of this book, whose title is another date: "1995-2002."

It gathers a few brief talks to responsible Jewish audiences, about the possible future of Catholic-Jewish relationships. Since the book was published in Europe, what was then simply a hope, or at least a fervent wish, has materialized far beyond whatever one could imagine.

An unpredictable combination of circumstances permitted the establishment of steady, trustful relationships between representatives of the Catholic hierarchy and leaders of the most fervent and rigorous Jewish orthodoxy.

What that Jewish orthodoxy actually means is barely known among the general public. In France at least, it hardly conjures up anything more than the picturesque inhabitants of the Mea Shearim neighorhood in Jerusalem. The existence of those Jewish communities is perceived essentially through their dress and diet, and also because they do not mix with the rest of the population. This is what is branded as "communitarianism" in Europe, and Jewish orthodoxy is supposed to be a particularly radical form of it.

In reality, this orthodoxy was mostly born in East European Jewish communities, which started a new life on the other side of the Atlantic, especially in the United States and principally in New York. Some of them came over very early, at the beginning of the twentieth century. Others crossed the ocean after World War II.

These groups have diversified priorities and styles, although they only make up a minority in American and world Judaism. But they are amazingly lively, and they offer something like a hoard of fervor and knowledge, or a store of faithfulness to Israel's religious vocation. Among them, as was the case in Germany in the first third of the twentieth century, some insisted on blending uncompromising faithfulness to the different schools of the Jewish tradition with bold participation in the venture of modernity — in the fields of thought, secular knowledge, and the social life.

These Jewish forms of orthodoxy have one thing in common: they avoid or even refuse any exchange on the subject of Christianity. This reserve is grounded in the memory of the tragedies, rejections, and persecutions of the past. But it also used to be based on the idea that Judaism had nothing to expect or ask from Christians as far as Jewish self-understanding is concerned.

Now, during the encounters I have just mentioned, Catholic theologians, bishops, and cardinals from several continents could acknowledge a change was taking place. I can point out three of its characteristic features.

1. Under the leadership of John Paul II, the Church has gone a long way toward retrieval of its Jewish roots. The Pope's gestures and statements, as well as his teachings on Christian-Jewish relationships, have made it possible to overcome a number of suspicions and misgivings that seemed unconquerable.

Restored mutual *confidence* makes possible — and along unprecedented lines — a dialogue that had never actually taken place in former centuries, even in the early history of Christianity.

Nothing of the past has been forgotten. But every suffering is borne in the acceptance of the truth. And that acknowledgment now bears witness to the Christians' disinterested friendship for and religious love of the Jewish people.

2. As a result, the ongoing relationship has taken up a new tone. The wounds and mistakes of the past cannot prevent the present from being different. The recovered and accepted consciousness of a common origin allows each side to rely on the other's sincerity and disinterestedness in the new relationship that has been initiated.

Of course, at the heart of this dialogue there remains a "Sign of Contradiction" — as the Gospel of Luke puts it — namely the person of Jesus, who for the Christians is the Messiah. But it appears that he is a sign *and* a contradiction that can no longer be overlooked at a time when what we have in common and what brings us together is being acknowledged.

3. On what can these new relationships be built? In spite of their obvious differences in religious culture, means of expression, and practices, orthodox Jews and Catholic pastors have found that they share a common language, which can be called that of *faith, prayer,* and *Scripture* — even if the Jewish and Catholic ways of receiving the latter within a tradition only partially coincide.

In any case, this spiritual communion is undeniable. It exists and survives even though the Sign of Contradiction stands out, even though we must grant Martin Buber's claim that the experience, the prayer, and the faith are not identical. But the convergence and communion are all the more manifest when both Jewish and Catholic believers become aware that they are immersed in the world of pagan secularism and cannot ignore it.

This was the heart of those encounters between Catholic leaders and those orthodox Jews who are often supposed to be most reluctant to engage in any kind of dialogue: we have acknowledged that we have *a common mission toward humanity.* This is because of the light that the Revelation casts upon the human condition. From the event of Creation to the gift of the Law, the Bible describes man's vocation and his spiritual nature in letters of fire. Such is our common legacy, as it was given to the Jewish people, from whom we Christians received it.

*   *   *

The new millennium does open up for the future new and so far unhoped-for possibilities of "dialogue." This may also mean "dispute," or even "contradiction," or "disagreement," depending on the translation of the adjective *antilegomenos* in Luke 2:34. But the word has been deprived of its polemical dimension, and rather remains a goad that turns our eyes toward the ultimate horizon of human history, as the hope for the Kingdom of God fills our hearts.

I am not sure whether these additional remarks may help those who will have read this book, or whether it will increase their uneasiness. I remain nevertheless grateful to the American publisher for giving me this opportunity.